Pick-Up Artist Lines of a Modern Casanova

Pick-Up Artist Lines of a Modern Casanova

333 Chat Up Lines for Men to Attract Their Dream Girl or a Fling for the Night

Be.Bull Publishing Group
Mauricio Vasquez
Toronto, Canada

Authors:
Be.Bull Publishing Group
Mauricio Vasquez

First Printing: December 2024

ISBN 978-1-998402-94-6 (Paperback)
ISBN 978-1-998402-96-0 (Hardcover)
ISBN 978-1-998402-95-3 (Ebook)

Introduction

Welcome to *Pick-Up Artist Lines of a Modern Casanova*, your essential guide to mastering the art of conversation and attraction.

In today's fast-paced world, making a memorable first impression is crucial, whether you're at a social event, on a dating app, or simply meeting someone new. This book equips you with a carefully curated collection of chat-up lines designed to captivate, charm, and create genuine connections.

Gone are the days when pick-up lines were dismissed as cheesy or ineffective. Successful interactions now rely on a blend of confidence, authenticity, and strategic communication. *Pick-Up Artist Lines of a Modern Casanova* transcends traditional dating advice by focusing solely on practical, impactful lines tailored for various situations— whether you aim to attract your dream girl or enjoy a memorable fling for the night.

Pick-up lines are more than just clever phrases—they are gateways to conversation, opportunities to showcase your personality, and tools to break the ice in situations that might otherwise feel intimidating. A well-timed, thoughtfully chosen line can ease tension, elicit a genuine smile, and open the door to deeper dialogue. The true power of a pick-up line lies not just in the words themselves but in the confidence and sincerity behind their delivery.

Inspired by the timeless charm of Casanova and refined with contemporary insights into interpersonal dynamics, this book offers a nuanced approach to attraction.

Confidence is the cornerstone of effective communication. By arming yourself with a repertoire of engaging lines, you prepare for spontaneous interactions and cultivate a sense of assurance that enhances all your social endeavors.

Embarking on the journey to elevate your dating game starts with investing in yourself and your ability to connect with others. *Pick-Up Artist Lines of a Modern Casanova* is more than just a collection of lines—it's a strategic toolkit for unlocking your potential as a confident, charismatic individual capable of forging meaningful relationships.

As you explore these pages, you'll discover the subtle art of balancing humor, charm, and sincerity, turning every interaction into an opportunity for connection.

Welcome to a new chapter of your social prowess. The power to connect, charm, and captivate is now in your hands.

Thank you for reading *Pick-Up Artist Lines of a Modern Casanova.* Want to excel in more aspects of your life?

Scan the QR code above to access my full range of books, designed to enhance your confidence, improve your relationships, and foster personal development.

Enjoyed the pick-up lines in *Pick-Up Artist Lines of a Modern Casanova?*

Let us know! Your reviews help others discover effective strategies and inspire us to create even better content.

Please take a moment to leave your feedback and support our community by scanning this QR code.

Thank you!

Table of Contents

Chapter 1. House Parties or Gatherings 10

Chapter 2. Cocktail Events / Formal Receptions 17

Chapter 3. Cultural Events (Art Shows, Museums, Galleries) 23

Chapter 4. Coffee Shops 29

Chapter 5. Lunch Breaks / Common Areas 35

Chapter 7. Gyms or Fitness Classes 47

Chapter 8. Workplace or Networking Events 53

Chapter 9. Seminars or Workshops 59

Chapter 10. Casual Bars and Lounges 66

Chapter 11. Dance Floors or Social Clubs 72

Chapter 12. Initial Messages when Dating 79

Chapter 13. Follow-Up Chats when Dating 85

Chapter 14. Commenting on Posts / Stories in Social Media 91

Chapter 15. Direct Messaging in Social Media 97

Chapter 16. Wedding Receptions 103

Chapter 17. Family or Friends' Milestone Celebrations 110

Chapter 18. Group Tours / Backpacking Hostels ... 116

Chapter 19. Airport Lounges or Waiting Areas 123

Chapter 20. Elevator Chats 129

Chapter 21. Public Transportation 135

Chapter 1. House Parties or Gatherings

Below you will find 16 compliments, conversation "hooks," and pick-up lines suited for a House Party or Gathering environment. These lines draw on humor, creativity, and genuine curiosity—helping you break the ice, spark a smile, and pave the way for more meaningful conversation.

1. Cheeky

Line: "I just saw you light up this room, so I had to come over and thank you for making the party brighter."

- Tone & Delivery: Smile warmly and deliver with playful warmth. Keep your voice relaxed and friendly.
- Adaptation: Use this after she's made someone laugh or shown a positive vibe. Emphasize genuine admiration rather than simple flattery.

2. Cheesy

Line: "Are you the music playlist here? Because every time I'm near you, the vibe gets better."

- Tone & Delivery: Keep a lighthearted, slightly exaggerated tone so she knows you're having fun. A tiny, good-natured eye-roll or grin acknowledges the cheesiness.
- Adaptation: Best used when there's actual music playing in the background. Tailor the line to reference the current song/genre to show attention to detail.

3. Corny

Line: "I'm starting to think this party was thrown just so I could meet you."

- Tone & Delivery: Lean into the "corny" factor with a playful smile. Show confidence; own the cliché.
- Adaptation: Ideal when you're introduced by a mutual friend or if the conversation naturally leads to how each of you got invited.

4. Flirty

Line: "I was looking for my friend, but got distracted by your smile—care to help me find them?"

- Tone & Delivery: Keep eye contact and a friendly grin, but don't overdo it. Use a gentle, curious tone.
- Adaptation: A natural way to strike up a conversation while moving around the party. Transition smoothly into small talk about mutual acquaintances or funny moments at the gathering.

5. Phone-Related

Line: "I was going to check my phone, but I realized I'd much rather talk to you instead."

- Tone & Delivery: Show authenticity in your voice.

Present the line as a genuine choice to engage with her, not a forced approach.

- Adaptation: Perfect if you see her momentarily on her phone or if you both just finished checking messages. It bridges from the digital world to the immediate, real-life moment.

6. Romantic

Line: "You have a presence that makes everything else fade out—how do you do that?"

- Tone & Delivery: Speak softly and with sincerity. This is more intimate, so gauge her comfort and personal space first.
- Adaptation: Best used in a quieter corner of the party. Show genuine curiosity about her rather than just a flashy line.

7. Rude

(Note: The "Rude" category is inherently risky, as it can offend or turn people off. If you choose to use it, employ caution, ensure the vibe is extremely playful, and that you've already established some rapport.)

Line: "You're way too captivating—everyone else here might be a little jealous that I stole all your attention."

- Tone & Delivery: Keep a mischievous yet smiling tone, making it sound more like banter than a genuine insult to others.
- Adaptation: Use only if she's clearly enjoying friendly teasing and has shown a playful side. If in doubt, go for gentler lines.

8. Crude

(Like "Rude," "Crude" lines can be off-putting without the right context or rapport. They're best reserved for situations where there's already a playful, cheeky dynamic established.)

Line: "You're causing a real problem here—I can't focus on anything else but you."

- Tone & Delivery: A wry smile and a soft chuckle can help it land as a flirtatious jibe instead of an overbearing remark.
- Adaptation: Make sure the overall party vibe is light, you're both in a joking mood, and that her reactions lean toward playful banter.

9. Weird

Line: "If we were aliens checking out Earth, you'd be the one I'd beam up first."

- Tone & Delivery: Ham it up. Show that you're aware it's offbeat, which can spark a laugh or at least a curious reaction.
- Adaptation: Works if she's got a quirky sense of humor, or if the party setting is already leaning into silliness or costumes/theme.

10. Lines Specifically for Women (to Use on Men or Other Interests)

Line: "I'm pretty sure you just stole my best dance move—care to show me how you did it so flawlessly?"

- Tone & Delivery: Lightly teasing. Smile with confidence.
- Adaptation: Perfect if the music is playing and you've noticed he's showing off some moves. It starts a

friendly challenge.

11. Cheeky Redux

Line: "I heard rumors that the coolest person here might be looking for a conversation partner. Should I let them know I found you?"

- Tone & Delivery: Light and playful, almost as if you're letting her in on a secret.
- Adaptation: Use when she's standing with a small group or alone, and you want to add a dash of humor to your approach.

12. Cheesy Redux

Line: "I think the DJ forgot to play the best track—your laughter. Any chance I could hear it again?"

- Tone & Delivery: A playful, half-joking voice. Acknowledge it's cheesy by smiling.
- Adaptation: Best timed after she laughs at something you or someone else said. Transitions nicely into further talk about music or party highlights.

13. Corny Redux

Line: "This place feels like a movie set, and clearly, you're the main character."

- Tone & Delivery: Warmth in your voice—like you're making a playful observation.
- Adaptation: Great if you're referencing the overall ambiance or vibe. Follow up with a question: "What's your storyline tonight?"

14. Flirty Redux

Line: "I can't decide which is more impressive—your style or your smile. Mind if I hang around to figure it out?"

- Tone & Delivery: Friendly confidence, direct eye contact, and a genuine smile.
- Adaptation: Use if she's dressed in a standout outfit or has an especially bright demeanor. Complimenting both style and aura signals that you appreciate more than just looks.

15. Phone-Related Redux

Line: "I'm collecting only the best party contacts tonight—mind if I start my list with yours?"

- Tone & Delivery: Lighthearted, with a slight wink in your tone. You're basically turning the act of exchanging numbers into a playful scenario.
- Adaptation: Use if you've already shared a moment or two of fun conversation. It doesn't feel rushed if you genuinely connected first.

16. Romantic Redux

Line: "You have a way of making the noise around us fade—like there's only you and me in the room."

- Tone & Delivery: Soft, sincere tone. Show genuine appreciation in your eyes.
- Adaptation: Better when the music or chatter is quite loud but you're standing close, so it feels personal, not forced.

Tips for Success

1. Gauge Her Receptiveness: Before delivering any line, observe her body language and mood. If she's deep in

conversation or visibly stressed, it may not be the right time.

2. Use Genuine Compliments: Authenticity goes a long way. If something truly strikes you about her (style, humor, confidence), craft your line around that.

3. Stay Light and Respectful: Even with cheeky or "weird" lines, keep the mood fun—avoid sounding intrusive or overly intense.

4. Transition Smoothly: After the initial line, ask open-ended questions to get to know her. This demonstrates genuine interest beyond a rehearsed opener.

5. Listen More Than You Speak: Connection grows when both parties engage. Keep your ears open for her responses, interests, and comfort level.

By blending these lines with respectful humor, awareness of context, and a sincere interest in the person you're speaking to, you'll strike the balance of confidence and warmth—true hallmarks of a modern-day Casanova in any house-party setting.

Chapter 2. Cocktail Events / Formal Receptions

Below you will find 16 compliments, conversation "hooks," and pick-up lines that suit a Cocktail Event or Formal Reception environment. These lines blend sophistication with a touch of playful charm, helping you ease into conversation while respecting the formal ambiance.

1. Cheeky

Line: "You carry yourself with such poise—I had to stop by and ask if you give lessons in elegance."

- Tone & Delivery: Light, playful tone with a refined demeanor. Smile and maintain polite eye contact.
- Adaptation: Perfect as an opener when you notice her confident presence in the room.

2. Cheesy

Line: "I was told this event would be full of brilliant minds and graceful people—seeing you, I understand why."

- Tone & Delivery: Keep a warm smile, subtly acknowledging the line is a bit "cheesy."
- Adaptation: Use when the conversation can flow easily into why you're both attending (networking, celebration, etc.).

3. Corny

Line: "I heard the most captivating person in the room would be here tonight. Now I see the rumors were absolutely true."

- Tone & Delivery: Own the corniness with a genuine grin. Let your eyes show friendly admiration.
- Adaptation: Best used if you've observed her enjoying herself—demonstrating a relaxed, inviting vibe.

4. Flirty

Line: "Formal events can be stiff, but your smile makes this whole evening feel effortlessly charming."

- Tone & Delivery: Speak with a confident, but not overpowering, tone. Lean in slightly to show genuine interest.
- Adaptation: Ideal if you catch her momentarily away from the crowd or in a quieter corner.

5. Phone-Related

Line: "I was about to check my email, but I realized I'd much rather check in on how you're enjoying the night."

- Tone & Delivery: Make it casual, as if you truly decided to engage with her instead of your phone.
- Adaptation: Great if you see her glance at her phone or if you both just finished replying to a message.

6. Romantic

Line: "Something about you has me picturing a classic waltz in a grand ballroom—do you mind if I share this dance in conversation?"

- Tone & Delivery: Gentle, quietly confident. Offer a polite smile that shows genuine interest in getting to know her.
- Adaptation: Use when there's soft music or a graceful atmosphere. If dancing isn't literal, segue into a lighthearted chat about music or the event.

7. Rude

Line: "I'm almost offended—no one warned me there'd be someone here who'd completely distract me from networking."

- Tone & Delivery: Slightly teasing, with a warm smile to soften any sharp edge.
- Adaptation: Make sure she's already smiling or laughing with you. The line should come across as fun, not aggressive.

8. Crude

Line: "I came here for business talk, but you're making me forget my entire elevator pitch."

- Tone & Delivery: Light-hearted chuckle to indicate self-awareness.
- Adaptation: Use after you've chatted a bit and want to interject playful honesty about how she's stealing your attention.

9. Weird

Line: "If this were a 1920s soiree, you'd be the Great Gatsby and I'd be sneaking in just to meet you."

- Tone & Delivery: Embrace the whimsical aspect, giving a small laugh to show you're in on the 'weirdness.'
- Adaptation: If the theme or style of the event is elegant or vintage-inspired, it can spark a fun literary or historical reference.

10. Lines Specifically for Women (to Use on Men or Other Interests)

Line: "I see you're charming everyone here—I had to find out if you're really this interesting or if it's just great PR."

- Tone & Delivery: Good-natured challenge, delivered with a confident smile.
- Adaptation: Perfect for a female attendee who notices a man commanding attention. This invites him to prove his genuine personality.

11. Cheeky Redux

Line: "I've been trying to figure out which is more impressive: your style or your confidence. Care to help me decide?"

- Tone & Delivery: A hint of curiosity, a polite smile.
- Adaptation: Use if she's particularly well-dressed or appears self-assured. You acknowledge both sophistication and personality.

12. Cheesy Redux

Line: "Forgive me, but when I saw you, I forgot the rest of the event's agenda. Could you remind me what we're celebrating?"

- Tone & Delivery: Deliver with a playful "oops" tone, as if you genuinely got distracted.
- Adaptation: Good if you two are near a sign or schedule for the event—turn it into humor about losing focus.

13. Corny Redux

Line: "I realized I don't need another cocktail. Talking to you is already lifting my spirits."

- Tone & Delivery: Friendly, with light emphasis on the pun.
- Adaptation: Ideal if she's holding a drink or if you just got yours. Smoothly transitions into chatting about favorite beverages or the event's catering.

14. Flirty Redux

Line: "There's an air of confidence about you that outshines even the chandeliers. Mind if I bask in it for a moment?"

- Tone & Delivery: Soft-spoken, warm, and direct.
- Adaptation: Suitable in a softly lit area or if the venue has noticeable, elegant lighting. Follow up with genuine questions about her interests.

15. Phone-Related Redux

Line: "I bet your contact list is just as classy as you are— what does someone have to do to earn a spot in it?"

- Tone & Delivery: Polite mischief, with a small grin.
- Adaptation: Use after some rapport; otherwise, it might seem too forward. Perfect if you've discussed business cards or networking.

16. Romantic Redux

Line: "The way you carry yourself... it's like you stepped out of an old Hollywood film. I'm honored to share the scene with you tonight."

- Tone & Delivery: Sincere, with respectful admiration.
- Adaptation: Best used when you've had a short exchange already and can sense she appreciates thoughtful compliments.

Tips for Success at a Formal Reception

1. Match the Sophistication of the Event: Keep your language polished and your demeanor respectful. Avoid anything overly brash or invasive.
2. Aim for Genuine Conversation: Transition quickly from your opener into meaningful dialogue about her interests or your shared reasons for attending.
3. Body Language & Pace: Cocktail events can be busy. Gauge if she has time or willingness to talk. Don't monopolize her attention if she's in the middle of networking.
4. Listen & Engage: After delivering your line, show real interest in her responses—ask about her background, the event itself, or mutual connections.

By pairing your suave approach with respect and sincerity, you'll stand out as the charming, emotionally intelligent modern-day Casanova who knows exactly how to navigate the polished atmosphere of a formal reception. Enjoy the conversation!

Chapter 3. Cultural Events (Art Shows, Museums, Galleries)

Below are 16 compliments, conversation "hooks," and pick-up lines that suit a Cultural Event—whether it's an Art Show, Museum, or Gallery. These lines leverage the creative, reflective atmosphere of cultural events to spark genuine conversations and memorable first impressions.

1. Cheeky

Line: "I'm trying to decide which masterpiece here is the most captivating... and I keep coming back to you."

- Tone & Delivery: Playful sincerity. Flash a light smile to show you're being genuine but not overly serious.
- Adaptation: Best used if she's visibly enjoying the exhibit, so it feels contextual rather than random flattery.

2. Cheesy

Line: "They say every painting tells a story, but I'm far more intrigued by what your story might be."

- Tone & Delivery: Warm, good-humored. Let your eyes express curiosity.
- Adaptation: Great after admiring a particular artwork together. Transition smoothly to asking about her own interests or favorite pieces.

3. Corny

Line: "I came here to appreciate art, but I think I just stumbled upon an even greater masterpiece standing right next to me."

- Tone & Delivery: Lean into the corny factor—smile and add a tiny shrug that says "I know it's cheesy, but I couldn't resist."
- Adaptation: Perfect when you both pause at a striking exhibit, and you want to pivot into a more personal conversation.

4. Flirty

Line: "I've seen countless works on these walls, yet somehow your presence is the most inspiring."

- Tone & Delivery: Soft-spoken, gentle confidence. Show genuine admiration in your eyes.
- Adaptation: Best delivered when you're discussing a piece or quietly sharing thoughts about the ambiance.

5. Phone-Related

Line: "I was about to snap a photo of this painting, but I'd rather remember this moment—especially meeting you—without a screen between us."

- Tone & Delivery: Sincere, with a slight chuckle as you put your phone away.
- Adaptation: Use if you catch yourself or her taking pictures. It signals genuine engagement and interest in a real conversation.

6. Romantic

Line: "In a room full of priceless art, your presence gives me the most vivid memory to take home."

- Tone & Delivery: Quiet admiration, soft eye contact.
- Adaptation: Works well during a slower moment at the gallery—when the crowd disperses or you find a calm corner to talk.

7. Rude

Line: "I can't believe they allowed something so distracting in here—you're making it impossible for me to focus on the art."

- Tone & Delivery: A half-smile or playful laugh ensures it's understood as a light tease, not an insult.
- Adaptation: Only use if there's already a rapport or a playful banter established.

8. Crude

Line: "It's unfair—they spent years creating these works, yet you stole my attention in seconds."

- Tone & Delivery: Dry humor, accompanied by a small grin.
- Adaptation: Make sure she's amused by the intensity of the statement; otherwise, tone it down or pivot to a safer line.

9. Weird

Line: "If this was an ancient Egyptian exhibit, I'd be convinced you were an undiscovered goddess."

- Tone & Delivery: Embrace the odd angle with a twinkle in your eye, indicating it's playful.
- Adaptation: Ideal if you're standing near historical or mythological art—like sculptures or artifacts from a past civilization.

10. Lines Specifically for Women (to Use on Men or Other Interests)

Line: "I'm curious—which piece is your favorite, or are you planning to steal the show yourself?"

- Tone & Delivery: Light challenge, confident but friendly.
- Adaptation: Great if he's really into the exhibit or noticeably passionate about certain pieces. You're inviting him to share and also teasing his ego a bit.

11. Cheeky Redux

Line: "I came in search of a deeper understanding of art... and I think you just gave it to me in one glance."

- Tone & Delivery: A soft grin and steady, friendly eye contact.
- Adaptation: Suited to a moment where you catch each other's eyes across an exhibit, prompting an inviting approach.

12. Cheesy Redux

Line: "They should frame this moment because meeting you is the real highlight of my day."

- Tone & Delivery: Warm, slightly self-aware—acknowledge the cheesiness with a smile.
- Adaptation: Perfect if you've chatted briefly and want to lighten the mood further.

13. Corny Redux

Line: "I'm feeling inspired to create something beautiful myself—maybe a story that starts with us meeting here."

- Tone & Delivery: Express genuine excitement, as though the environment truly sparked your imagination.
- Adaptation: Use when discussing how art can inspire new ideas or if she's mentioned being creative herself.

14. Flirty Redux

Line: "Your insights about this piece are captivating—I feel like I'm seeing the art through your eyes, and I love the view."

- Tone & Delivery: Genuine appreciation in your voice.
- Adaptation: If she shared her perspective on a particular artwork, highlight her intelligence and unique interpretation.

15. Phone-Related Redux

Line: "I'd love to compare notes on our favorite pieces—maybe we can swap phone numbers and continue this tour together."

- Tone & Delivery: Polite, friendly confidence.

- Adaptation: Use after you've had a brief discussion about the art. This is a natural pivot to staying connected.

16. Romantic Redux

Line: "Surrounded by centuries of creativity, it's refreshing to meet someone who feels like a modern masterpiece."

- Tone & Delivery: Gentle, reflecting admiration in your expression.
- Adaptation: Best delivered in a quiet or dimly lit section of the exhibit, where the mood feels more intimate.

Tips for Success at Art Shows, Museums, or Galleries

1. Show Genuine Interest: Ask about her opinions on the art. Listen actively, showing curiosity for her perspective.
2. Match the Atmosphere: Most cultural events are relatively calm. Maintain a respectful volume and composure.
3. Use Open-Ended Questions: Invite her to describe what she sees, feels, or thinks. This not only validates her opinion but also keeps the conversation natural.
4. Offer Your Own Insights: If you have a genuine reaction to a piece or know something interesting about it, share it. Showcasing a bit of knowledge can create a deeper connection.
5. Keep It Respectful: Cultural venues often come with certain etiquette—avoid being loud or disruptive to other attendees.

By weaving these lines with active listening and genuine engagement, you'll craft an authentic, respectful connection in a refined yet playful way—truly worthy of a modern-day Casanova in any cultural setting.

Chapter 4. Coffee Shops

Below are 16 carefully selected compliments, conversation "hooks," and pick-up lines suitable for Coffee Shops. These lines leverage the relaxed, inviting vibe of coffee shops— where you can easily strike up a conversation about the drinks, ambiance, or that intriguing book you notice in her hands.

1. Cheeky

Line: "The aroma in here is amazing, but I think you just brewed up a new level of delightful."

- Tone & Delivery: Light, playful, and friendly. Let a small grin show you're genuinely complimenting her.
- Adaptation: Perfect if you catch her enjoying a specialty coffee. You're playfully comparing the café's ambiance to how captivating she is.

2. Cheesy

Line: "I asked the barista for something sweet; I had no idea I'd run into you."

- Tone & Delivery: Warm smile, slightly self-aware of the cheesiness.
- Adaptation: Ideal after you've received your drink or if you're both standing in line. It's a quick, easy way to break the ice and share a laugh.

3. Corny

Line: "I just realized that coffee beans aren't the only thing here that's grounded and warm—you seem that way too."

- Tone & Delivery: Lighthearted with a gentle tone; deliver it as an endearing pun.
- Adaptation: Works best if she gives off a calm, friendly vibe. You're linking her demeanor to the comfortable coffee-shop environment.

4. Flirty

Line: "I came in for a caffeine boost, but your smile might be the real energy kick I needed."

- Tone & Delivery: Softly spoken with a confident but not overpowering demeanor.
- Adaptation: Great if she's genuinely smiling or in a cheerful mood. Acknowledge her positive energy without being overly forward.

5. Phone-Related

Line: "I was about to check my messages, but then I noticed you, and suddenly my phone seems far less interesting."

- Tone & Delivery: Genuine with a tinge of amusement, as if you're surprised by how easily she caught your attention.
- Adaptation: Perfect if you or she was just on the phone; it shows you'd rather be present in the moment with her.

6. Romantic

Line: "Your presence feels like a cozy corner on a rainy day—peaceful, warm, and exactly where I'd like to stay."

- Tone & Delivery: Quiet sincerity, soft eye contact.
- Adaptation: Best delivered when the atmosphere is mellow—like a weekend morning or a calm weekday afternoon. It resonates with the comforting vibe of a coffee shop.

7. Rude

Line: "You're making this place dangerously distracting—how's anyone supposed to focus on their coffee?"

- Tone & Delivery: Slight grin, light tease. Make it obvious you're joking.
- Adaptation: Suited if there's a mutual playful energy or if she's already engaged in some fun banter with you.

8. Crude

Line: "This coffee shop is known for strong brews, but your presence is the real knockout here."

- Tone & Delivery: Keep it confident yet friendly—avoid any aggressive undertone.

- Adaptation: If she seems open to a bold joke, present it with a light chuckle to ease any shock factor.

9. Weird

Line: "If aliens landed here right now, I'd tell them you're the human they absolutely have to meet."

- Tone & Delivery: Emphasize the silliness, smiling or softly laughing at your own line.
- Adaptation: Good if she appears to appreciate quirky humor (e.g., reading a sci-fi book or wearing something whimsical).

10. Lines Specifically for Women (to Use on Men or Other Interests)

Line: "You seem as refreshing as a cold brew on a hot day—mind if I get a sample of your conversation?"

- Tone & Delivery: Confident, slightly teasing.
- Adaptation: Great if he's sipping on a unique drink or discussing it with someone. Lets you smoothly dive into conversation about preferences and tastes.

11. Cheeky Redux

Line: "The latte art here is good, but it's nothing compared to the masterpiece of you."

- Tone & Delivery: Soft smile, playful but polite.
- Adaptation: Ideal if you notice she's admiring her latte or if the café is known for fancy latte art.

12. Cheesy Redux

Line: "I asked the barista if they had a pick-me-up more effective than espresso—turns out, it's talking to you."

- Tone & Delivery: Gently playful, letting her in on the joke.
- Adaptation: Especially good if she comments on needing an energy boost or you're both yawning about an early morning.

13. Corny Redux

Line: "I'm convinced this cappuccino foam was poured just right so I'd have the courage to say hi to you."

- Tone & Delivery: Present it like a casual confession, relaxed body language.
- Adaptation: Works as a quick opener if you're both at the bar waiting for drinks, highlighting a fun coincidence.

14. Flirty Redux

Line: "I thought caffeine was addictive, but your smile might just be my new favorite fix."

- Tone & Delivery: A friendly glint in your eye, letting her see it's genuine flattery.
- Adaptation: Use if she's genuinely smiling or laughing about something—preferably after you've shared a quick friendly moment.

15. Phone-Related Redux

Line: "I've got a loyalty card for this place, but can I earn some points chatting with you instead?"

- Tone & Delivery: Light and humorous, as though you're spontaneously thinking it up.
- Adaptation: Great if you see she's using a rewards card or if you're paying together at the counter.

16. Romantic Redux

Line: "The best conversations happen over coffee. I'd love to start one with you, if you'll let me."

- Tone & Delivery: Warm, open sincerity—like you're genuinely interested in knowing her story.
- Adaptation: Use this after making eye contact or exchanging a brief smile. It's an easy, inviting pivot to sit down together.

Tips for Success in Coffee Shops

1. Observe the Vibe: Notice if she's relaxed, reading, or in a hurry. Approach gently if she's focused or busy, and always be respectful of her space.
2. Bring Genuine Curiosity: If she has a unique drink or a book, use that as a starting point. Show real interest in her taste or hobby.
3. Time It Right: If she's engrossed in her laptop or headphones, wait until there's a natural pause. A friendly wave or smile first can help gauge receptiveness.
4. Use Light Conversation Starters: After your opener, transition to more personal but not overly invasive topics—like favorite coffee blends, local cafés, or travel stories.
5. Stay Respectful: If she doesn't seem interested or is giving short responses, gracefully bow out. A modern-day Casanova respects boundaries and vibes.

By weaving these lines with genuine interest and a respectful approach, you'll create a comfortable, friendly atmosphere—perfect for turning that chance coffee-shop encounter into a pleasant memory (or even something more). Enjoy your next latte moment!

Chapter 5. Lunch Breaks / Common Areas

Below are 16 carefully curated compliments, hooks for attraction, and pick-up lines fitting a Lunch Break or Common Area context—whether at work, on a campus, or in a communal space. These lines are playful, yet respectful—ideal for those shared midday moments when everyone is looking to relax and recharge.

1. Cheeky

Line: "Your smile does more for my appetite than anything from the lunch menu."

- Tone & Delivery: Light, playful tone with a bright smile to mirror the positivity.
- Adaptation: Perfect if you spot her looking upbeat. It subtly highlights you appreciate her vibe over the

food.

2. Cheesy

Line: "I'm torn between grabbing a bite or just savoring this moment with you—mind if I choose both?"

- Tone & Delivery: Warm, slightly exaggerated sincerity, acknowledging the cheesiness with a grin.
- Adaptation: Good for when you both have a bit of time and you're looking to share a quick chat while waiting in line for food or coffee.

3. Corny

Line: "I'm wondering if the secret ingredient in your lunch is charm—because you brought plenty of it here."

- Tone & Delivery: Good-natured and softly enthusiastic.
- Adaptation: If she has something interesting or homemade, it's a gentle way to comment on how she lights up the space.

4. Flirty

Line: "I'm convinced this afternoon just got brighter the moment you walked in—who knew lunch breaks could be this exciting?"

- Tone & Delivery: Smooth confidence without overpowering; maintain friendly eye contact.
- Adaptation: Use if the atmosphere is slightly bustling but you two share a moment of eye contact.

5. Phone-Related

Line: "I was about to scroll through social media, but then I realized talking to you in real life would be way more interesting."

- Tone & Delivery: Genuine, with a mild laugh, as though you're pleasantly surprised by her presence.
- Adaptation: Great if you were both on your phones or she's wrapping up a quick call.

6. Romantic

Line: "Between the everyday rush and deadlines, meeting you feels like an unexpected breath of fresh air."

- Tone & Delivery: Sincere, gentle voice. Let your expression reflect genuine appreciation.
- Adaptation: Works well in a quieter corner, such as a lunchroom window seat or a hallway, where you can momentarily escape the crowd.

7. Rude

Line: "This lunch break was supposed to be my relaxation time—then you showed up and totally distracted me."

- Tone & Delivery: Smile or a light chuckle so she knows you're kidding around.
- Adaptation: Only if you've exchanged a few words or smiles already. Make sure she's comfortable with friendly banter.

8. Crude

Line: "I'm not sure if it's hunger or pure fascination, but my heart's definitely racing right now."

- Tone & Delivery: Lighthearted, with a wink or grin to show it's a bold but friendly statement.
- Adaptation: If she's been joking or bantering with you, it can be a fun (albeit bold) way to express interest.

9. Weird

Line: "If lunch breaks are the 'twilight zone' of the workday, you're definitely the highlight cameo I didn't expect."

- Tone & Delivery: Embrace the quirky factor—smile and deliver with a playful nod to its strangeness.
- Adaptation: Ideal for someone who seems to appreciate offbeat humor (maybe referencing pop culture or has a quirky T-shirt).

10. Lines Specifically for Women (to Use on Men or Other Interests)

Line: "Hey, I'm doing an informal survey: Do guys like chatting with someone intriguing on their lunch break? Because you're looking pretty intriguing."

- Tone & Delivery: Friendly confidence, a hint of playful curiosity.
- Adaptation: Perfect if you catch him off guard—then smoothly shift the conversation into more natural topics like work, food, or shared interests.

11. Cheeky Redux

Line: "I used to think coffee was my midday perk, but seeing you just gave me a boost no espresso ever could."

- Tone & Delivery: Light and easygoing, with a quick flash of a smile.

- Adaptation: If she's sipping on coffee or you're near the coffee machine, it's a fun way to tie in the setting.

12. Cheesy Redux

Line: "I could have ordered takeout, but there's no way Uber Eats delivers this kind of charm."

- Tone & Delivery: Let her see you're fully aware it's a playful exaggeration.
- Adaptation: Ideal when a food delivery came in or if people are talking about lunch options—you pivot it to appreciate her presence.

13. Corny Redux

Line: "I didn't think the highlight of my day would be found in the lunchroom, but here you are, proving me wrong."

- Tone & Delivery: Warm honesty, but let a little playful grin show you're fully acknowledging the corniness.
- Adaptation: Works if you just casually bumped into her, reinforcing the idea that serendipity brought you together.

14. Flirty Redux

Line: "I'm trying to decide which is more appealing—this lunch spread or the spark in your eyes."

- Tone & Delivery: Soft, direct eye contact. Smile with genuine admiration.
- Adaptation: Perfect if she's glancing at you or you two have locked eyes briefly across the table or seating area.

15. Phone-Related Redux

Line: "Mind if I trade my lunch hour screen-time for a conversation with the most interesting person in the room?"

- Tone & Delivery: Genuine, slightly upbeat.
- Adaptation: If you see her scrolling on her phone, show that you'd prefer real human interaction over digital distractions.

16. Romantic Redux

Line: "Amid the buzz of work life, meeting you feels like an oasis in a desert. Do you mind if I linger a while?"

- Tone & Delivery: Sincere, calm, and friendly.
- Adaptation: Use this if there's a relatively quiet moment in the break area. It sets a gentle, warm atmosphere.

Tips for Success in Lunch/Common Areas

1. Respect the Pace: Lunchtime can be short. Gauge if she's in a hurry. If she seems rushed, keep it brief and non-intrusive.
2. Connect Over Shared Space: Since you're both there to eat or take a break, use that common ground to strike up a conversation about favorite dishes, restaurants, or funny workplace/campus anecdotes.
3. Emphasize Politeness: Be mindful of boundaries—some might just want a quiet break. Watch for open body language or eye contact before delivering your line.
4. Smooth Follow-Up: After your opener, ask a simple, genuine question. For example, "What's your go-to lunch spot around here?" or "Any favorite break-time activities?"

5. Keep It Friendly: A modern-day Casanova respects someone's personal space and reacts graciously if she's not interested in conversation.

By combining these lines with genuine listening skills and empathy for the other person's midday pace, you'll be well on your way to turning casual lunch breaks into delightful connections. Enjoy your conversation!

Chapter 6. Parks and Recreational Spaces

Below are 16 carefully crafted compliments, conversation openers, and pick-up lines that work well in Parks and Recreational Spaces—whether you're near a lake, strolling a garden, or enjoying a weekend picnic. Use these lines with a friendly demeanor, respect for personal space, and genuine curiosity about the person you're approaching.

1. Cheeky

Line: "I came here for fresh air, but it looks like you're the real breath of fresh air in this park."

- Tone & Delivery: Light, playful warmth with a friendly

smile.

- Adaptation: Perfect if she's leisurely strolling or sitting on a bench, simply enjoying the scenery. Acknowledge the park's peaceful vibe before delivering the line.

2. Cheesy

Line: "I thought nature was the most beautiful thing here—until I saw you."

- Tone & Delivery: Deliver with gentle humor and a grin that conveys, "I know this is cheesy, but it's sincere."
- Adaptation: Works best if you're both admiring a scenic view or flower garden; you transition from appreciating nature to appreciating her presence.

3. Corny

Line: "I must be lost, because your smile is taking me down a trail I wasn't expecting to follow."

- Tone & Delivery: Warm, slightly self-aware. Let a small laugh show you're in on the corny factor.
- Adaptation: Good if you literally just stumbled onto her path or happen to be near a nature trail. Let the environment inspire the line.

4. Flirty

Line: "Do you have a map? I keep losing my way whenever I glance into your eyes."

- Tone & Delivery: Soft-spoken, confident, and playful.
- Adaptation: Best used if there's already a friendly vibe. Maybe you've exchanged a few smiles or she's

given you a welcoming look.

5. Phone-Related

Line: "I was about to check my weather app, but it's obvious you're the sunshine lighting up this park."

- Tone & Delivery: Good-natured, with an easygoing chuckle.
- Adaptation: Perfect if you or she had her phone out or mentioned the weather. It's a fun pivot to personal engagement over screen time.

6. Romantic

Line: "Some people come here to escape the city noise. Me? I think I found my peace right here talking to you."

- Tone & Delivery: Gentle, softly spoken, with genuine admiration.
- Adaptation: Ideal if you've started a short conversation about how the park is a quiet retreat. Keep the moment calm and intimate.

7. Rude

Line: "You're seriously messing with my quiet time—how am I supposed to relax when you're this distracting?"

- Tone & Delivery: Light tease, accompanied by a friendly grin that clarifies you're not actually annoyed.
- Adaptation: Only suitable if she's been joking around or you've shared a playful moment. Avoid if she's enjoying solitude.

8. Crude

Line: "I came out here to clear my head, but you're stirring up more excitement than I can handle."

- Tone & Delivery: Subtle, wry smile to keep it light.
- Adaptation: Only attempt if she's already shown a playful sense of humor and there's clear mutual interest.

9. Weird

Line: "If squirrels could talk, they'd tell me to get over here and say hi to you already."

- Tone & Delivery: A playful, quirky tone—slight grin to show you realize it's offbeat.
- Adaptation: Ideal if you actually see squirrels or if she's feeding birds. It's whimsical and disarming.

10. Lines Specifically for Women (to Use on Men or Other Interests)

Line: "You blend in here perfectly—strong, calm, and a part of the scenery. Mind if I join you for a moment?"

- Tone & Delivery: Confident, direct, but with a welcoming smile.
- Adaptation: Great if he's leaning against a tree or simply taking in the view, looking relaxed and content.

11. Cheeky Redux

Line: "They should rename this spot 'You Park,' because you just took my attention away from everything else."

- Tone & Delivery: Lighthearted, with a little shrug to show it's a playful exaggeration.

- Adaptation: Good for a moment of friendly eye contact that sparks curiosity.

12. Cheesy Redux

Line: "I don't know which is more refreshing today—this breeze or meeting you."

- Tone & Delivery: Warm smile, a hint of playful charm.
- Adaptation: Especially fitting if there's a gentle breeze or weather changes to comment on.

13. Corny Redux

Line: "I heard connecting with nature can boost happiness… but I think connecting with you has it beat."

- Tone & Delivery: Softly spoken; own the corniness with genuine positivity.
- Adaptation: Perfect if she's actively enjoying nature (jogging, meditating, or just people-watching).

14. Flirty Redux

Line: "I was enjoying the scenery, then you appeared and made the day so much brighter. Mind if I soak up your company for a bit?"

- Tone & Delivery: Warm, direct, but with gentle eye contact.
- Adaptation: Use if the vibe is open and friendly— maybe she's smiled at you or you've both paused near a scenic overlook.

15. Phone-Related Redux

Line: "I was about to check my steps count for the day, but somehow my heart's racing more from chatting with you."

- Tone & Delivery: Amused sincerity, lightly playful.
- Adaptation: Best if you notice she's taking a walk or you're both out for a jog. It references fitness in a fun way.

16. Romantic Redux

Line: "Standing here with nature all around, it feels like the world slowed down just so we could have this moment."

- Tone & Delivery: Soft, genuine, as though you're sharing a heartfelt observation.
- Adaptation: Works wonderfully at a more serene spot—by a pond, under a tree, or near a scenic overlook—where you can both pause and take in the view.

Tips for Success in Parks & Recreational Spaces

1. Be Mindful of Personal Space: Parks often give people a sense of calm or solitude. Approach gently and gauge her receptiveness to conversation.
2. Use the Environment: Notice if she's walking a dog, reading, or just relaxing. Show genuine interest in that activity to start an organic exchange.
3. Keep It Casual: Parks are laid-back settings. Start with easygoing remarks before moving to more personal topics.
4. Watch Body Language: If she seems immersed in nature or uninterested, respect that. If she's receptive, maintain open body language and a comfortable speaking distance.
5. Stay Authentic: A modern-day Casanova knows

confidence and sincerity triumph over forced lines. Adapt your approach to what feels natural.

By pairing these lines with genuine warmth and a respect for the peaceful setting, you'll create a friendly, inviting atmosphere perfect for forging new connections under the open sky. Enjoy your stroll!

Chapter 7. Gyms or Fitness Classes

Below are 16 carefully curated compliments, conversation hooks, and pick-up lines tailored for a Gym or Fitness Class setting. Use these lines with genuine confidence, an awareness of personal boundaries, and an interest in her workout goals or fitness journey.

1. Cheeky

Line: "I was going to blame my racing heart on the treadmill, but I think it has more to do with you."

- Tone & Delivery: A playful grin, warm tone.

- Adaptation: Perfect if you both just finished running or are on nearby cardio machines. Keeps things light and fun.

2. Cheesy

Line: "I came here to lift weights, but seeing you just lifted my entire mood."

- Tone & Delivery: Slightly self-aware smile; own the cheesiness.
- Adaptation: Ideal as a quick opener when you cross paths near the free weights or machines.

3. Corny

Line: "I can't decide what's stronger—these dumbbells or the impression you just made on me."

- Tone & Delivery: Friendly, with a small laugh at the pun.
- Adaptation: Works if you're sharing the same equipment area or waiting for a bench; break the ice with humor.

4. Flirty

Line: "I heard endorphins make people happier—watching you work out might be the reason I'm smiling so much right now."

- Tone & Delivery: Soft-spoken, easy confidence.
- Adaptation: Best if you've already shared a passing glance or quick smile, so it feels natural, not random.

5. Phone-Related

Line: "I was about to check my workout app, but I realized chatting with you might be the real progress I need today."

- Tone & Delivery: Slight humor, genuine interest.
- Adaptation: Use it if you see her pause to check her phone, or if you're both reviewing an exercise plan.

6. Romantic

Line: "In a place full of people pushing their limits, you quietly stand out—like the calm in the middle of all this hustle."

- Tone & Delivery: Gentle sincerity; not too loud in the busy gym environment.
- Adaptation: Ideal if she exudes a focused, composed vibe. Approach when she's resting or hydrating between sets.

7. Rude

Line: "Your workout is making the rest of us look lazy. Could you slow down a second so I can say hi?"

- Tone & Delivery: Good-natured chuckle to show it's a friendly tease.
- Adaptation: Only if she's pushing herself hard and you sense an upbeat energy. Make sure your tone is clearly joking.

8. Crude

Line: "I'll be honest: I'm not sure if it's my muscles trembling or if you're just that distracting."

- Tone & Delivery: A wry smile, keep it confident but not

leering.

- Adaptation: Only use if there's clear mutual banter going on. Otherwise, go for a gentler approach.

9. Weird

Line: "If aliens landed right now, I'd point them to you and say, 'That's peak human performance—study her, not me.'"

- Tone & Delivery: Quirky, lighthearted, with an amused grin to show you're aware it's unusual.
- Adaptation: Fun if you both appreciate random humor or if she's mentioned anything sci-fi or unique.

10. Lines Specifically for Women (to Use on Men or Other Interests)

Line: "I noticed your form is on point—any chance you can spot me with some expert advice?"

- Tone & Delivery: Confident and straightforward.
- Adaptation: Great for striking up conversation with someone who appears knowledgeable or is doing a routine you admire.

11. Cheeky Redux

Line: "You must be a personal trainer, because just looking at you makes me want to up my fitness game."

- Tone & Delivery: Slightly playful, friendly.
- Adaptation: If she's doing an impressive exercise or looks exceptionally fit, offer this as a light compliment.

12. Cheesy Redux

Line: "I read that working out releases endorphins. Meeting you might've just doubled my dose for the day."

- Tone & Delivery: Friendly, with a knowing nod to the cheesiness.
- Adaptation: Use post-workout or after class, when everyone's in a good mood.

13. Corny Redux

Line: "We might be lifting weights, but the real heavy-lifter here is the interest you just sparked in me."

- Tone & Delivery: Warm, letting her see you're not afraid to be a bit silly.
- Adaptation: Perfect if you're both finishing a set or wiping down equipment.

14. Flirty Redux

Line: "I've been told to focus on my form, but I can't help noticing how flawless yours is—mind if I join your routine for a bit?"

- Tone & Delivery: Friendly invitation, not pushy.
- Adaptation: Works if she's open to having a gym buddy. Gauge her response; if she's comfortable, you can keep the conversation going.

15. Phone-Related Redux

Line: "I'm logging my reps—any chance I could log your number too, so we can compare workout tips?"

- Tone & Delivery: Casual, upbeat.
- Adaptation: Perfect if you've discussed fitness apps or

are comparing routines. It's a natural transition to staying in touch.

16. Romantic Redux

Line: "In a room filled with people chasing personal goals, meeting you feels like the best accomplishment of my day."

- Tone & Delivery: Sincere, with direct eye contact.
- Adaptation: Better delivered during a water break or class cooldown, where the noise level is lower and you can talk softly.

Tips for Success in Gyms & Fitness Classes

1. Respect Personal Space & Focus: People often have headphones in or are in the zone. Approach politely, ideally between sets or after class.
2. Compliment Effort, Not Just Appearance: Recognize her hard work and dedication—people appreciate praise for their discipline and motivation.
3. Stay Mindful of Hygiene & Etiquette: Wait until she's not mid-exercise. Keep the environment clean (wiping equipment, etc.), showing respect for the shared space.
4. Offer Help Only if Appropriate: If she's struggling or looks open to assistance, offer gently. But don't assume she needs it—always ask first.
5. Follow Her Lead: If her responses are short or she seems eager to return to her workout, gracefully exit. A modern-day Casanova recognizes boundaries.

By coupling these lines with genuine respect for her fitness journey and a thoughtful approach, you'll stand out as someone who's both charming and considerate. Enjoy your workout—and best of luck forging connections on and off the treadmill!

Chapter 8. Workplace or Networking Events

Below are 16 carefully crafted compliments, conversation openers, and pick-up lines appropriate for a Workplace or Networking Event. Because these events often involve professional settings, subtlety and respect are key. Always keep the context and corporate etiquette in mind.

1. Cheeky

Line: "I heard this place was buzzing with talent. Now that I see you, it makes perfect sense."

- Tone & Delivery: Warm smile, a gentle nod to the corporate atmosphere.
- Adaptation: Ideal when you meet someone new who clearly has a strong professional presence. It celebrates her competence as well as her presence.

2. Cheesy

Line: "I came here to network, but I'm secretly hoping we can connect on more than just LinkedIn."

- Tone & Delivery: Light, friendly, and just a bit playful—make it clear you're being tongue-in-cheek.
- Adaptation: Great after you've exchanged cards or LinkedIn details. It lightly hints at genuine interest without overstepping boundaries.

3. Corny

Line: "They said to find synergy at this event—I think the real synergy is happening right here, chatting with you."

- Tone & Delivery: Keep it casual, with a small laugh to acknowledge the corporate jargon turned personal.
- Adaptation: Suited to a moment where you both joke about "office buzzwords." It's a humorous pivot from professional to personal.

4. Flirty

Line: "Your confidence in that meeting was impressive—care to share where you get that fearless spark?"

- Tone & Delivery: Admirative but genuine. Show real curiosity rather than just flattery.
- Adaptation: Use if you've observed her speaking or presenting. It transitions naturally into a conversation about her career path or interests.

5. Phone-Related

Line: "I was about to check my emails, but then I saw you walk in and realized there's someone far more interesting to follow up with."

- Tone & Delivery: Polite, with a small smile that shows

you're putting away your phone.

- Adaptation: Perfect if you both have phones in hand. It frames your interest as more intriguing than any digital ping.

6. Romantic

Line: "Your poise in this professional setting feels like a secret superpower—makes me wonder what other incredible talents you're hiding."

- Tone & Delivery: Soft-spoken, appreciative. Emphasize genuine interest in her abilities and personality.
- Adaptation: Deliver this one-on-one, in a quieter corner of the event rather than in front of colleagues.

7. Rude

Line: "I thought I was prepared for everything at this event, but you just threw me off my game—care to explain yourself?"

- Tone & Delivery: With a light laugh and a raised eyebrow, indicating it's harmless teasing.
- Adaptation: Only if there's a clear, playful back-and-forth already established. Otherwise, it can sound confrontational.

8. Crude

Line: "They promised me refreshments here, but I'm finding you far more refreshing than any cocktail they're serving."

- Tone & Delivery: Slight grin, confident but still respectful.
- Adaptation: If the atmosphere loosens up and you

both have a drink in hand, it can land as bold but charming. If in doubt, opt for a safer line.

9. Weird

Line: "If this were a corporate universe, you'd be the star around which all these conversations orbit. Mind if I join your orbit for a moment?"

- Tone & Delivery: Embrace the quirkiness; a soft smile to show it's intended to be fun.
- Adaptation: Works if she's the center of attention or has a charismatic presence. It's a playful way to compliment her social gravity.

10. Lines Specifically for Women (to Use on Men or Other Interests)

Line: "That presentation of yours was so impressive I might just have to bribe you with coffee for more insights. Are you open to being persuaded?"

- Tone & Delivery: Confident, slightly playful.
- Adaptation: Transition from complimenting his professional skills to a casual suggestion of coffee or a chat outside the formal event.

11. Cheeky Redux

Line: "I heard you're the go-to person for brilliant ideas, but you didn't warn me how easy it'd be to get hooked on your conversation."

- Tone & Delivery: Congenial, with a friendly smirk.
- Adaptation: Best used if you've already exchanged a few interesting thoughts and sense mutual

engagement.

12. Cheesy Redux

Line: "I was certain I'd just be exchanging business cards tonight, but now I'm hoping to exchange something more meaningful—like stories or even future plans."

- Tone & Delivery: Acknowledge the cheese factor with a small laugh, but keep eye contact sincere.
- Adaptation: Perfect if you've already traded cards, giving you a reason to deepen the connection.

13. Corny Redux

Line: "We're supposed to make impactful introductions, right? Well, consider me impacted—meeting you just stole the spotlight."

- Tone & Delivery: Warm, slightly playful.
- Adaptation: Ideal if you just met her and felt an instant connection. Reflect that enthusiasm kindly, not overwhelmingly.

14. Flirty Redux

Line: "I can't decide what's more impressive—your professional accomplishments or the intriguing spark in your eyes. Care to enlighten me?"

- Tone & Delivery: Compliment her achievements first, then transition to a personal note.
- Adaptation: Works if she's recently mentioned a project or success. Balances respect for her work and genuine interest in her as a person.

15. Phone-Related Redux

Line: "I'm typically glued to my phone at these events, but you've got me genuinely present in the moment—how do you do that?"

- Tone & Delivery: Friendly, slightly amazed.
- Adaptation: Use if you both just finished scanning your phones or are exchanging LinkedIn info. Shifts focus back to real conversation.

16. Romantic Redux

Line: "I came expecting another routine networking night, but your presence has added something extraordinary to the mix—I'd love to know more about you."

- Tone & Delivery: Soft sincerity, respectful admiration in your voice.
- Adaptation: Deliver when the conversation naturally shifts to personal backgrounds or life interests beyond work.

Tips for Success at Workplace or Networking Events

1. Prioritize Professionalism:Compliment her skills, style, or insights before venturing into more personal territory.
2. Observe the Setting: If it's a formal corporate event, keep your tone subtle. If it's a relaxed after-work social, you can be a bit more playful.
3. Read Her Body Language: If she seems rushed or focused on networking for business, adapt accordingly. Offer to follow up later instead of forcing a longer chat.
4. Transition Naturally: Start with professional

conversation or shared industry topics, then pivot to something more personal if she seems interested.

5. Offer a Next Step: Suggest coffee or a LinkedIn connection if you sense a spark. Keep it respectful, with an easy out if she's uninterested.

A modern-day Casanova in the workplace or networking scene knows the value of confidence tempered by professionalism and genuine respect. By blending these lines with sincere interest in her expertise and outlook, you'll stand out effortlessly—no awkwardness required. Good luck!

Chapter 9. Seminars or Workshops

Below are 16 carefully selected compliments, conversation starters, and pick-up lines suitable for Seminars or Workshops. Because these events are often educational or professional, a warm, genuinely curious approach will resonate more than aggressive or overly bold lines. Let your interest in the subject matter—and in her perspective—shine through naturally.

1. Cheeky

Line: "I came here to learn something new, but I didn't expect my biggest takeaway to be meeting someone as intriguing as you."

- Tone & Delivery: Light, friendly, with a relaxed smile—acknowledge it's a bit playful.
- Adaptation: Perfect after a short discussion about the seminar's topic. Show you value her presence and unique viewpoint.

2. Cheesy

Line: "They said this workshop would expand my mind; they forgot to mention it might also steal my heart."

- Tone & Delivery: A warm grin, letting her know you're aware it's a tad over-the-top.
- Adaptation: Use only if there's already a hint of mutual humor or banter. Best delivered when you've shared a laugh or two.

3. Corny

Line: "I was looking for inspiration in today's session—but one glance at you, and I'm brimming with new ideas already."

- Tone & Delivery: Soft chuckle or half-smile to showcase you're in on the corniness.
- Adaptation: Great for a moment when she's just shared an insight or question, highlighting her contribution.

4. Flirty

Line: "Your questions during the session were as captivating as you are—any chance I could hear more of your brilliant thoughts later?"

- Tone & Delivery: A sincere compliment on her insight, delivered with casual confidence.
- Adaptation: Perfect if she's asked an interesting question that caught your attention. Transition naturally into inviting her for a follow-up chat.

5. Phone-Related

Line: "I was about to check my notes on my phone, but somehow I'm more curious about getting your perspective on this topic. Care to share?"

- Tone & Delivery: Gentle, genuinely inquisitive, reflecting that you value her input.
- Adaptation: If you both have your phones out, you pivot from typical phone-checking to real human connection.

6. Romantic

Line: "Amid all these slides and speeches, the only moment that truly resonated with me was when our eyes met."

- Tone & Delivery: Quiet sincerity, a mild, respectful smile—avoid being too dramatic in a professional setting.
- Adaptation: Use in a calm moment, perhaps during a break when there's space for a softer, more personal note.

7. Rude

Line: "You seriously expect me to concentrate on the lecture with someone this distracting in the room?"

- Tone & Delivery: Light, teasing, with a good-natured grin that shows you're joking.
- Adaptation: Only if you've already established some rapport or playful banter—otherwise, it might feel off-putting.

8. Crude

(High risk in a formal setting—only if the vibe is clearly open to bolder humor.)

Line: "I thought I'd be overloaded with info, but it's you who's got me overloaded with excitement."

- Tone & Delivery: Keep it somewhat subtle and delivered with a friendly grin.
- Adaptation: Possibly okay for a more informal or interactive workshop. Gauge her comfort level before trying something this forward.

9. Weird

Line: "If I used a flowchart to trace the best outcomes of this workshop, it'd lead me straight to this conversation with you."

- Tone & Delivery: A playful or nerdy self-awareness—smile as you reference "flowcharts."
- Adaptation: Fun if the seminar uses diagrams or is about problem-solving. Embrace the quirky side lightly.

10. Lines Specifically for Women (to Use on Men or Other Interests)

Line: "That was quite the clever comment you made. Does that sharp mind come with a coffee chat option? Because I'd love to pick it."

- Tone & Delivery: Confident, with a matter-of-fact approach that still feels friendly.
- Adaptation: Perfect for acknowledging someone's intelligence and proposing a casual follow-up outside the seminar setting.

11. Cheeky Redux

Line: "I thought the highlight of this workshop would be the keynote speaker—turns out, it's the moment I got to say hi to you."

- Tone & Delivery: Soft, playful sincerity, accompanied by an easy smile.
- Adaptation: Ideal for initiating conversation after a break or Q&A session, bridging from the event to a personal connection.

12. Cheesy Redux

Line: "I keep trying to focus on the seminar, but it's tough when you're the most enlightening thing in the room."

- Tone & Delivery: Let her see your slight grin, acknowledging it's deliberately cheesy.
- Adaptation: Use it if you sense she's up for a little humor and you're in a more relaxed part of the event.

13. Corny Redux

Line: "I came to expand my professional network, but I think the only connection I want right now is yours."

- Tone & Delivery: Friendly, leaning in slightly to show genuine interest.

- Adaptation: Works after some light conversation about networking—segue into something more personal.

14. Flirty Redux

Line: "I've heard knowledge is power, but meeting you feels like the real game-changer today."

- Tone & Delivery: Calm, direct, appreciative.
- Adaptation: If she's shared interesting insights or if you've both contributed to a discussion, acknowledge her impact.

15. Phone-Related Redux

Line: "I was going to snap pictures of the slides, but maybe I should snap your details instead—seems way more worth revisiting."

- Tone & Delivery: Light, friendly, with a slightly amused tone, as if it just occurred to you.
- Adaptation: A natural pivot if you've been taking photos of slides or if others are exchanging contact info.

16. Romantic Redux

Line: "All these notes will help my career, but your presence here is the note I'll cherish most. Could we compare takeaways over coffee?"

- Tone & Delivery: Quiet and genuine—respectful of her personal space and time.
- Adaptation: Perfect after the final session, when you both have time to reflect on the content (and each

other).

Tips for Success at Seminars & Workshops

1. Highlight Her Intellectual Contributions: Seminars are learning environments. Show genuine interest in her perspectives or questions.
2. Stay Professional Yet Personable: Maintain a respectful tone—she's there to learn, not just be approached. Make sure your line feels natural, not forced.
3. Observe Body Language: If she's engaged in a group conversation or taking diligent notes, wait for an appropriate break. Gauge her readiness to chat.
4. Segway from Event Content: Start by discussing the seminar topic or something the speaker said—then pivot to a more personal connection if she's receptive.
5. Follow Up Casually: If the conversation flows well, suggest exchanging contact info or continuing the discussion over coffee. Keep it light, polite, and optional.

A modern-day Casanova at a seminar or workshop skillfully blends sincere admiration for her intellect with respectful social cues—turning a structured learning environment into a stepping stone for deeper, more meaningful connection. Enjoy discovering new insights together, both academically and personally!

Chapter 10. Casual Bars and Lounges

Below are 16 carefully tailored compliments, hooks for attraction, or pick-up lines suited for a Casual Bar or Lounge setting. Whether it's a cozy bar with dim lighting or a lively lounge with upbeat music, the key is to read her body language, pace, and vibe—so you can complement her evening rather than disrupt it.

1. Cheeky

Line: "I thought the best thing on the menu here was the cocktails—turns out it's actually your company."

- Tone & Delivery: Warm and playful, with a small smile or nod to acknowledge you're flirty without being pushy.
- Adaptation: Perfect if she's checking out the drink list; pivot from discussing the bar's menu to complimenting her presence.

2. Cheesy

Line: "I asked the bartender for something sweet. He pointed to you."

- Tone & Delivery: Slightly self-aware, delivered with a friendly grin that says, "I know this is cheesy, but it's fun!"
- Adaptation: Great if you're near the bar and the conversation naturally leads to the subject of sweet or signature cocktails.

3. Corny

Line: "I came here to unwind, but I think I just found the most relaxing spot—right next to you."

- Tone & Delivery: Soft chuckle, letting her see you're leaning into the corniness.
- Adaptation: Use when she appears relaxed or is enjoying the lounge's ambiance, reinforcing the idea that her presence is comforting.

4. Flirty

Line: "I know the lighting is dim, but you're still the brightest thing in this room."

- Tone & Delivery: Confident, but not overbearing—speak softly so it feels personal.
- Adaptation: Ideal if she's in a corner, under ambient lighting, or if there's a warm vibe you can reference.

5. Phone-Related

Line: "I was about to scroll through my socials, but something tells me talking to you would be way more interesting."

- Tone & Delivery: Genuine, friendly, with a slight laugh

to show it's a spontaneous thought.

- Adaptation: Perfect if you or she has a phone out. It's an easy pivot from digital distractions to real-life connection.

6. Romantic

Line: "In a place filled with chatter and music, your voice is the only sound I'm really drawn to hear more of."

- Tone & Delivery: Warm sincerity, gentle eye contact, slightly leaned in as you speak.
- Adaptation: Use if you've already exchanged a few words or you've overheard her say something intriguing.

7. Rude

Line: "I tried to relax tonight, but you're making it impossible to focus on anything else—care to explain yourself?"

- Tone & Delivery: Light teasing, small grin, and soft laugh to clarify it's not an actual complaint.
- Adaptation: Only if there's mutual banter and she seems to enjoy playful jokes

8. Crude

Line: "Not sure if it's the drinks or just you, but I'm feeling buzzed from your energy already."

- Tone & Delivery: A mischievous smile but keep it friendly—avoid any appearance of pushing boundaries.
- Adaptation: Appropriate if the conversation has a fun, edgy vibe. If uncertain, opt for a more subtle approach.

9. Weird

Line: "If this bar were a spaceship, you'd be the captain—I just got pulled in by your magnetic field."

- Tone & Delivery: Quirky grin, showing you're fully aware it's a silly analogy.
- Adaptation: Works if she seems to appreciate offbeat humor or you spot something hinting at a fun personality (e.g., a sci-fi T-shirt).

10. Lines Specifically for Women (to Use on Men or Other Interests)

Line: "I've been told I'm a good judge of character—and my instincts say you're worth a second round of conversation."

- Tone & Delivery: Confident, cool, but not aloof.
- Adaptation: Great if you've exchanged a couple of lines or jokes already, indicating you'd like to continue getting to know him.

11. Cheeky Redux

Line: "You're making the playlist in here sound even better—like you bring your own rhythm to the room."

- Tone & Delivery: Lighthearted, referencing the music or atmosphere.
- Adaptation: Use if she's casually moving to the beat or seems to really enjoy the background music.

12. Cheesy Redux

Line: "I came for happy hour, but seeing you, I'd say the 'happy' part just leveled up."

- Tone & Delivery: Friendly and jovial, as though you really are having a more enjoyable night.
- Adaptation: Perfect if the bar has a specific happy hour vibe or sign posted, and you want to reference it playfully.

13. Corny Redux

Line: "I'm collecting stories tonight, and you seem like the most interesting chapter I could dive into."

- Tone & Delivery: Warm, curious tone—make it sound like you genuinely want to hear her story.
- Adaptation: Use if she mentioned something unique, or if you sense she has an intriguing background or vibe.

14. Flirty Redux

Line: "That sparkle in your eye is more potent than anything the bartender could ever mix—care to share your secret recipe?"

- Tone & Delivery: Playful, a bit whimsical, as if you're genuinely captivated.
- Adaptation: Great if she's looking at you with interest or has a natural brightness in her expression.

15. Phone-Related Redux

Line: "Everyone's snapping photos here, but I'd rather capture this moment in my memory—especially if it ends with me getting to know you better."

- Tone & Delivery: Slightly sentimental, with a soft smile.
- Adaptation: Ideal if people around are taking selfies

or pictures of their drinks, and you want a more personal approach.

16. Romantic Redux

Line: "For a place filled with chatter and clinking glasses, time seems to slow down whenever I catch your eye."

- Tone & Delivery: Gentle, sincere. Look into her eyes, but don't stare intensely.
- Adaptation: Best delivered in a quieter corner or after you've exchanged a few pleasant smiles or short remarks.

Tips for Success in Casual Bars & Lounges

1. Read the Room: Bars can be lively or chill. Gauge if she's open to conversation (eye contact, friendly body language) before diving in.
2. Watch the Volume: Music or chatter might be loud—lean in slightly and speak clearly, but don't invade personal space.
3. Be Authentic: If a line feels forced, pivot to something more natural like a comment on the music, décor, or vibe.
4. Offer Space: If she's not engaging or seems focused on her group, gracefully step back. Respect is key to leaving a positive impression.
5. Follow Up with Real Conversation: A good line breaks the ice. Next, ask open-ended questions or listen to her stories. True charm is in how well you engage, not just the opener.

When delivered with friendly confidence and genuine curiosity, these lines can spark everything from a fun conversation to a memorable connection—turning an ordinary lounge outing into a potentially unforgettable encounter. Enjoy meeting new people!

Chapter 11. Dance Floors or Social Clubs

Below are 16 compliments, hooks for attraction, or pick-up lines tailored for a Dance Floor or Social Club environment. In a high-energy atmosphere, timing and body language are crucial. Keep your approach light, fun, and respectful—let her see that you appreciate the vibe and are genuinely curious to know her.

1. Cheeky

Line: "I came here to dance, but I didn't realize the real showstopper would be you."

- Tone & Delivery: Light, playful, with an easy smile to show genuine warmth.
- Adaptation: Works well when you see her enjoying the music or commanding attention on the dance floor.

2. Cheesy

Line: "I asked the DJ for something that'd make my night unforgettable. Then I spotted you—mission accomplished."

- Tone & Delivery: Deliver with a grin that acknowledges the cheesiness.
- Adaptation: Good for a moment when you catch her eye or if she's near the DJ booth, blending the music reference with the compliment.

3. Corny

Line: "I might need a map—every time you move, I lose my sense of direction."

- Tone & Delivery: Soft chuckle or warm smile, letting her see you're aware it's a playful exaggeration.
- Adaptation: If she's dancing in a crowd, this can be a fun way to break the ice, hinting that she stands out from everyone else.

4. Flirty

Line: "The dance floor's crowded, but you're the only person I seem to notice. Think we can change that?"

- Tone & Delivery: Bold yet friendly—slightly lean in to ensure she hears you over the music.
- Adaptation: Perfect if you've shared glances while dancing. It's a direct, confident approach to invite her to dance with you.

5. Phone-Related

Line: "I was about to capture the energy of this place on my phone, but something tells me creating memories with you would be even better."

- Tone & Delivery: Genuine, as if you spontaneously decided that experiencing the moment is more important than recording it.
- Adaptation: Use this if you or she has just taken out a phone to snap a pic or video, transitioning smoothly into personal engagement.

6. Romantic

Line: "Between the lights and the bass, I feel like I'm lost in a dream—one that just got more beautiful when I saw you."

- Tone & Delivery: Soft, with a gentle smile—don't shout; move closer so it feels more intimate.
- Adaptation: Ideal if the music has a dreamy or atmospheric vibe. Wait for a quieter moment or a slowdown in the set.

7. Rude

(Use caution—ensure it's clearly playful, not genuinely harsh.)

Line: "I'm trying to concentrate on my moves, but you're making it impossible. Seriously, how am I supposed to keep my cool with you around?"

- Tone & Delivery: Light, teasing grin—make sure your body language shows admiration, not annoyance.
- Adaptation: Best if you've already established a fun back-and-forth. It can come off as a flirty challenge when done right.

8. Crude

(High risk on a dance floor. Only use if you sense a playful, edgy vibe.)

Line: "I can't tell if it's the music or you that's got my heart racing, but I'm guessing it's 90% you."

- Tone & Delivery: Semi-serious with a hint of amusement. Show you're leaning into a bold statement but not crossing lines.
- Adaptation: Works in a more high-energy club atmosphere where playful banter is common. Check for reciprocated interest.

9. Weird

Line: "If this club turned into a sci-fi movie, I'd bet all the aliens would be studying your moves before heading back to their planet."

- Tone & Delivery: Embrace the offbeat humor with a playful smile—show that you're being intentionally quirky.
- Adaptation: Use if she seems to have a fun, quirky style or if there's something whimsical about the event theme or costumes.

10. Lines Specifically for Women (to Use on Men or Other Interests)

Line: "You look like someone who's too cool to let this great music go to waste. Care to show me what you've got on the dance floor?"

- Tone & Delivery: Self-assured, slightly daring, but friendly.
- Adaptation: Perfect if you see him casually bobbing his

head or seeming ready to dance but not making the first move.

11. Cheeky Redux

Line: "I've seen a lot of dancers tonight, but your style has got me seriously rethinking my two-step game."

- Tone & Delivery: Friendly admiration, acknowledging you might need help with your own moves.
- Adaptation: Great if she's got distinct or impressive dance moves. You're showing genuine interest in her skill.

12. Cheesy Redux

Line: "I asked the bartender for the best drink recommendation; turns out, the real refreshment is dancing with you."

- Tone & Delivery: Accompanied by a playful eye roll or grin so she knows you're in on the cheese.
- Adaptation: Ties together the bar vibe and a direct compliment, bridging from your beverage situation to an invitation to dance.

13. Corny Redux

Line: "They say dancing is a conversation without words—mind if I learn your language tonight?"

- Tone & Delivery: Softly spoken, a warm smile to convey sincerity.
- Adaptation: Ideal for a slower tempo track or a moment when she's clearly enjoying the beat.

14. Flirty Redux

Line: "Your energy on this floor is contagious. I'm ready to catch it if you let me join your orbit."

- Tone & Delivery: Lighthearted, a slight lean-in to be heard over the music.
- Adaptation: Use if she's in a lively mood, clearly drawing attention with her dancing or positive energy.

15. Phone-Related Redux

Line: "Before I pull out my phone to post about this amazing night, I'd love to say hi in real time—care for a dance or two?"

- Tone & Delivery: Genuine and a bit spontaneous, as if you decided connecting in person is more important.
- Adaptation: Best if she's also on her phone or taking photos. It's a prompt to switch from virtual sharing to real-life interaction.

16. Romantic Redux

Line: "I'd say you move like a dream, but you're making me feel more awake than ever. Care if I join in?"

- Tone & Delivery: Intimate yet playful, pitched so she can hear you clearly.
- Adaptation: Good for slower songs or calmer moments in the music, setting a more romantic mood.

Tips for Success on Dance Floors & Social Clubs

1. Respect Personal Space: Clubs can be crowded, but always approach gently. Make eye contact before

moving close.

2. Lead with Fun: The atmosphere is about music and letting go—keep your energy light, positive, and inviting.

3. Watch for Cues: If she's fully immersed in the music or dancing with friends, time your approach to a natural break or mutual glance.

4. Encourage a Shared Experience: Focus on dancing together or enjoying the moment, rather than delivering lengthy monologues.

5. Offer a Smooth Exit: If she's uninterested, politely step back and wish her a great night. Classy exits maintain your respect and charm.

With a friendly smile, an open approach, and a respectful read of her interest, these lines can help create fun moments on the dance floor—potentially leading to a memorable connection well beyond the last song of the night. Enjoy the rhythm and the conversation!

Chapter 12. Initial Messages when Dating

Below are 16 tailored openers and compliments designed specifically for Initial Messages when Dating—whether it's on a dating app or the early stages of chatting via text. Since these are your first interactions, aim for a balance between fun, sincerity, and polite curiosity. Show genuine interest in who she is rather than treating her like just another match.

1. Cheeky

Line: "I was just scrolling through, minding my own business, and then—bam—you happened. Care to explain how you made my day so quickly?"

- Tone & Delivery: Warm, playful. Use a subtle wink or an emoji to keep it light (\uD83D\uDE09).
- Adaptation: Perfect for a first message that references how her profile caught your eye. Lets her know she stands out.

2. Cheesy

Line: "I've heard good conversations can brighten a whole day. Would you mind making mine absolutely radiant?"

- Tone & Delivery: Add a friendly, slightly self-aware tone—acknowledge it's a bit over the top.
- Adaptation: Use if her profile vibe suggests she likes positivity or romantic gestures. It's a warm opener that's less aggressive than some lines.

3. Corny

Line: "I'm on a mission to find the coolest person in this app. I have a strong feeling the quest ends with you."

- Tone & Delivery: Casual confidence. A small chuckle or smiling emoji to show you're in on the joke.
- Adaptation: Great if her profile or pictures radiate a fun, humorous energy. It's mildly flattering and sets a curious tone.

4. Flirty

Line: "I'm torn between complimenting your amazing profile and asking you how soon I can hear your laugh in person—any preferences?"

- Tone & Delivery: Friendly yet confident. It's direct but still polite.
- Adaptation: Ideal if she has a line in her bio about her sense of humor, or you sense she appreciates boldness.

5. Phone-Related

Line: "My phone said '15% battery left,' but somehow I'm sure a conversation with you could recharge me instantly."

- Tone & Delivery: Light humor, maybe a winking face or playful emoji (\uD83D\uDE0A).
- Adaptation: Makes a casual joke about phone usage. Good for someone who's obviously active on the app or has phone-related details in her bio.

6. Romantic

Line: "Sometimes, all it takes is one spark to ignite a great story. Care to see if this could be ours?"

- Tone & Delivery: Soft, warm approach—sincere but not overly intense.
- Adaptation: Use if her profile hints that she's open to deeper connections or is a bit of a romantic. It's an invitation, not a demand.

7. Rude

Line: "I was planning on quietly browsing profiles, but you just had to show up and ruin my plan by being so distractingly awesome."

- Tone & Delivery: Make sure it's tongue-in-cheek— maybe add a smirking emoji (\uD83D\uDE0F) to clarify you're joking.
- Adaptation: Only if her profile suggests she enjoys banter or sarcasm. Otherwise, it might come off as off-putting.

8. Crude

Line: "I'm trying to keep it classy here, but your profile is making it really hard to focus on anything else."

- Tone & Delivery: Edgy but keep it from sounding

disrespectful or vulgar.

- Adaptation: If her bio and photos exude a sassy or overtly playful style, you can risk it. Otherwise, it may offend.

9. Weird

Line: "If we were in a sci-fi movie, I'd be the alien determined to learn your secrets—care to reveal a few?"

- Tone & Delivery: A playful, almost nerdy charm. An alien or UFO emoji (\uD83D\uDE80) could emphasize the fun.
- Adaptation: Great if she's into quirky humor, fandoms, or references pop culture in her bio.

10. Lines Specifically for Women (to Use on Men or Other Interests)

Line: "A quick poll: what's your superpower? Because I'm sensing heroic levels of charisma from your profile."

- Tone & Delivery: Confident, direct. Possibly add a winking or strong arm emoji (\uD83D\uDCAA).
- Adaptation: Ideal to flip the script and show a playful yet self-assured vibe when you're the one initiating.

11. Cheeky Redux

Line: "My day was missing something, and I just realized—it was a conversation with you."

- Tone & Delivery: Enthusiastic yet casual.
- Adaptation: Good if her profile hints she's also seeking genuine connection. It's breezy and optimistic.

12. Cheesy Redux

Line: "I used to think perfect matches were a myth—your profile has me reconsidering."

- Tone & Delivery: Soft, sweet. Acknowledge the line's cheesiness with a little emoji or tone.
- Adaptation: Works well if she seems open to light flattery and classic romantic tropes.

13. Corny Redux

Line: "Who knew a simple swipe could lead me to someone who seems this intriguing?"

- Tone & Delivery: Friendly and curious—like you genuinely want to discover more about her.
- Adaptation: References the app context, bridging the gap between casual swiping and sincere interest.

14. Flirty Redux

Line: "I noticed you have quite a smile. Any chance you'd let me earn a few more of those?"

- Tone & Delivery: Warm and open. Let her know you appreciate positive energy.
- Adaptation: Works especially if her photos highlight a bright or playful smile—acknowledges a standout trait.

15. Phone-Related Redux

Line: "My phone suggested I take a break, but how can I when there's someone like you waiting on the other side?"

- Tone & Delivery: Lighthearted with a small laugh. Possibly add a shrug emoji (\uD83D\uDE05).
- Adaptation: Good if you're referencing digital burnout

or if she's hinted at minimal screen time. It's a polite way to prioritize her conversation.

16. Romantic Redux

Line: "They say every great story starts with a hello. Here's hoping ours becomes a page-turner."

- Tone & Delivery: Sincere, a touch whimsical. Let your genuine interest show.
- Adaptation: Ideal if you've read something in her profile indicating she enjoys books, storytelling, or creativity.

Tips for Success with Initial Messages

1. Personalize When Possible: If her profile mentions specific hobbies or interests, reference them to show genuine curiosity.
2. Keep It Light: Early interactions should feel fun, not heavy. Save deeper topics for later when rapport is established.
3. Mind Emojis & Tone: Text can be misread. A well-placed emoji or a short clarifying phrase helps convey warmth or playfulness.
4. Ask Open-Ended Questions: After your opener, invite her to share something about herself. "What drew you to [x interest]?" is more engaging than a yes/no question.
5. Respect Boundaries & Pace: If she takes a while to reply or seems cautious, don't push. Show understanding—real connections take time.

By combining these openers with genuine interest and respect for her uniqueness, you'll make a strong first impression—setting the stage for an enjoyable conversation that could lead to something special. Happy chatting!

Chapter 13. Follow-Up Chats when Dating

Below are 16 carefully chosen compliments, hooks for attraction, or pick-up lines to use during Follow-Up Chats when Dating—after that initial conversation is already underway. These lines are designed to deepen rapport, maintain momentum, and show sustained interest in getting to know her better.

1. Cheeky

Line: "You know, this conversation is starting to feel like my favorite show—hard to pause and always leaving me wanting the next episode."

- Tone & Delivery: Light and playful, with a smiling undertone to show genuine excitement.
- Adaptation: Great if you've had a few fun back-and-forth chats already. Positions her as someone you look forward to "tuning into."

2. Cheesy

Line: "I was just thinking: my day feels 10x brighter since we started chatting. Care to be my sunshine a bit longer?"

- Tone & Delivery: Soft, warm, and slightly tongue-in-cheek to acknowledge the cheese factor.
- Adaptation: Perfect for text conversations—especially if she's into sweet or romantic gestures.

3. Corny

Line: "I tried to come up with a witty line, but all I can think about is how fun it is to talk to you."

- Tone & Delivery: Genuine, with a small laugh or shrug.
- Adaptation: Works well if she appreciates honesty and a humble approach. Emphasizes that you value the connection over fancy lines.

4. Flirty

Line: "Your last message just made me smile in a way no emoji could ever capture—how do you manage that?"

- Tone & Delivery: Slightly teasing, but admiring.
- Adaptation: Great for letting her know you truly enjoy her style or humor. Keeps the vibe warm and intimate.

5. Phone-Related

Line: "I promised myself I'd put my phone down—but then your name popped up, and well... so much for self-control."

- Tone & Delivery: Lighthearted confession, a small chuckle in tone.
- Adaptation: Wonderful if you're texting late at night or if she knows you have a busy schedule. Shows she's a welcome distraction.

6. Romantic

Line: "It's funny how words on a screen can feel so real—talking to you is like a glimpse of something I'd love to see in person."

- Tone & Delivery: Soft, reflective. Keep it gentle, not overly dramatic.
- Adaptation: Use if your chats are deepening, and you sense real chemistry. Hinting you'd enjoy meeting if she's open to it.

7. Rude

Line: "I was actually productive until your message came in... now my focus is completely shot, so thanks a lot!"

- Tone & Delivery: A joking sigh or rolling-eyes emoji to clarify you're teasing.
- Adaptation: Only if she's shown she enjoys banter and can dish it back. Otherwise, it could land poorly.

8. Crude

Line: "I was going to say something clever, but you've already scrambled my brain. Not fair, but I'll take it."

- Tone & Delivery: Bold but keep the overall vibe playful.
- Adaptation: If your dynamic already includes flirty or daring jokes, this can work. Otherwise, err on a safer side.

9. Weird

Line: "If our convo was an alien invasion, I'd volunteer for further study—somehow, you're beaming down all the right signals."

- Tone & Delivery: Quirky, with a small laugh to show you're aware it's offbeat.
- Adaptation: Ideal if she's hinted at liking sci-fi, fantasy, or just a fun, unique sense of humor.

10. Lines Specifically for Women (to Use on Men or Other Interests)

Line: "I have this theory that interesting guys are rare. Care to prove me right again with a little more conversation?"

- Tone & Delivery: Confident, inviting.
- Adaptation: Flips the script by complimenting him while still prompting him to show more of his personality.

11. Cheeky Redux

Line: "I was about to share some random fact with you, but I realized you're the most intriguing 'fact' I've discovered recently."

- Tone & Delivery: Mildly flirtatious, with playful curiosity.
- Adaptation: Good if you've been swapping fun facts or random trivia. Pivots from a factual approach to a personal compliment.

12. Cheesy Redux

Line: "Every time my phone buzzes, I secretly hope it's you. Pretty sure my phone is jealous."

- Tone & Delivery: Friendly, affectionate, but aware it's a bit lovey-dovey.
- Adaptation: Perfect once you've established a friendly

texting pattern, showing you truly anticipate her messages.

13. Corny Redux

Line: "I tried describing your vibe to a friend, but words failed me—must be because you're too remarkable for a simple summary."

- Tone & Delivery: Sincere, with a hint of amazement.
- Adaptation: If she's shown multiple facets of her personality—be it humor, kindness, intellect—this line respectfully highlights her complexity.

14. Flirty Redux

Line: "When our conversation goes quiet, it feels like someone turned off the best song on the playlist. Let's hit 'play' again?"

- Tone & Delivery: Light, upbeat. Possibly add a music note emoji (\u266B).
- Adaptation: Great if you share a passion for music or if there was a lull in the chat. Sparks a new wave of discussion.

15. Phone-Related Redux

Line: "I just realized I scrolled through every meme in my feed without cracking a smile—probably because you weren't the one sending them."

- Tone & Delivery: Playful, comedic.
- Adaptation: Use if you two joke around often or send memes/gifs back and forth. It shows you miss her brand of humor.

16. Romantic Redux

Line: "It's amazing how a few messages from you can shift my day from ordinary to something worth remembering."

- Tone & Delivery: Heartfelt, letting sincerity shine through.
- Adaptation: Ideal if she consistently brightens your mood. Gently signals deeper affection or appreciation.

Tips for Success in Follow-Up Chats

1. Personalize to Her: Refer back to something she mentioned earlier—her hobbies, a funny moment, or her day's highlight. It shows active listening.
2. Balance Humor & Depth: Mix light banter with occasional meaningful questions. Avoid nonstop jokes or endless seriousness.
3. Encourage Back-and-Forth: End with a prompt or question inviting her to respond. "What do you think about that?" or "How's your week been treating you?"
4. Gauge Frequency: If she's responding energetically, match her pace. If she's slower, respect that—quality over quantity.
5. Aim for Natural Progression: As chats continue, move from surface-level topics to more personal stories, letting trust and comfort build organically.

By weaving these lines and tips into your follow-up chats, you'll convey genuine interest, emotional intelligence, and a spark of fun that keeps her looking forward to every message. Enjoy exploring deeper connections!

Chapter 14. Commenting on Posts / Stories in Social Media

Below are 16 tailored compliments, conversation hooks, and pick-up lines for Commenting on Posts / Stories on Social Media. Because social media can blur context (tone, emojis, etc.), be mindful of how your words might be interpreted. When possible, personalize your comment to something she posted—demonstrating genuine interest rather than a copy-paste line.

1. Cheeky

Comment: "I was scrolling mindlessly until your post popped up—then I realized my day was missing your spark."

- Tone & Delivery: Light, playful, acknowledging her post as the day's highlight.
- Adaptation: Perfect if her post is especially eye-catching. Show you're pleasantly surprised, not just tossing generic flattery.

2. Cheesy

Comment: "This post made my heart skip a beat—was that the vibe you were going for, or is that just your natural talent?"

- Tone & Delivery: Warm, slightly over-the-top but in a friendly way.
- Adaptation: Great if the photo or caption is particularly striking. Acknowledge it might be cheesy by pairing it with a playful emoji (\uD83D\uDE09).

3. Corny

Comment: "Your post just convinced me that some smiles can outshine any filter—this might be Exhibit A."

- Tone & Delivery: Genuine enthusiasm, letting her know you recognize her smile or happy vibe is the real star.
- Adaptation: Use if she's smiling in the pic or shares something uplifting. Keeps the focus on her positivity.

4. Flirty

Comment: "Your sense of style and captions are always on point—but I think the real masterpiece is your confidence shining through."

- Tone & Delivery: Complimentary, referencing both her aesthetic and underlying self-assuredness.
- Adaptation: Ideal if she consistently posts stylish outfits or has a knack for witty captions.

5. Phone-Related

Comment: "I got lost in notifications, but your story just pulled me back to reality—thanks for that (and for looking amazing)."

- Tone & Delivery: Mix of gratitude and admiration,

lightly referencing phone use.

- Adaptation: Good if you see her story after missing multiple alerts; it shows you're genuinely intrigued by her content.

6. Romantic

Comment: "It's incredible how a single photo or snippet of your day can feel so enchanting—I might need a full storytime soon."

- Tone & Delivery: Soft, interested, hinting at wanting more depth.
- Adaptation: Use when her post piques real curiosity about her experiences. It's a gentle invite to share more.

7. Rude

Comment: "Thanks for making me rethink my productivity—here I am stuck, mesmerized by your post instead of working."

- Tone & Delivery: Light teasing. Possibly add a laughing or shrug emoji to clarify it's a joke (\uD83D\uDE05).
- Adaptation: Only if she appreciates banter or you've joked around before. Avoid if you're unsure she'll receive it well.

8. Crude

Comment: "Well, I was trying to keep it classy here, but your post is making me think all sorts of distractions."

- Tone & Delivery: Bold but not vulgar; let a flirtatious undertone show.

- Adaptation: If her post has a playful or provocative edge and you know she won't mind an edgier vibe.

9. Weird

Comment: "If aliens asked me what 'awesome' looks like, I'd just point them to this post of yours."

- Tone & Delivery: Quirky, fun, acknowledging it's a bit out there.
- Adaptation: Good if she has a playful personality, or if the post is imaginative, cosplay-oriented, or otherwise unique.

10. Lines Specifically for Women (to Use on Men or Other Interests)

Comment: "Your post is basically my new motivation board—mind if I borrow some of that confidence?"

- Tone & Delivery: Confident but appreciative, inviting further banter.
- Adaptation: Perfect if his post showcases an achievement or a positive mindset you find inspiring.

11. Cheeky Redux

Comment: "I used to think my feed was fun until your post showed me what real excitement looks like."

- Tone & Delivery: Friendly smirk, a bit of a wink in text form (\uD83D\uDE09).
- Adaptation: Works if her content stands out for creativity, humor, or an energetic vibe.

12. Cheesy Redux

Comment: "This might sound cheesy, but your post is the highlight of my entire scrolling session."

- Tone & Delivery: A playful confession, acknowledging the cheesiness.
- Adaptation: Keep it short and sweet to ensure it doesn't feel heavy-handed.

13. Corny Redux

Comment: "I was trying to find something witty to say, but honestly, your post speaks louder than any witty line ever could."

- Tone & Delivery: Simple admiration, lightly self-deprecating about failing to be witty.
- Adaptation: Great if the post has a deeper message or a strong visual component worth praising.

14. Flirty Redux

Comment: "Scrolling just got infinitely better—mind if I lock in this vibe and keep it for a while?"

- Tone & Delivery: Playful, with a dash of direct flirtation.
- Adaptation: Ideal if you sense her post aims to spread positivity or a feel-good mood.

15. Phone-Related Redux

Comment: "I was about to put my phone away, but then I saw your update. Guess my screen time's about to increase, and I'm not mad about it."

- Tone & Delivery: Lighthearted, referencing personal

phone habits.

- Adaptation: Good for when you've been offline for a bit or you're acknowledging you can't resist seeing her newest post.

16. Romantic Redux

Comment: "Seeing life through your lens is like stepping into a brighter world—thank you for that glow."

- Tone & Delivery: Soft, heartfelt, appreciating the perspective her content brings.
- Adaptation: Perfect if her posts have a positive, uplifting theme. Gently hints you'd like to see more of her worldview.

Tips for Success in Social Media Comments

1. Context is Key: Reference something specific in her post or story—like the location, caption, or an activity—to show genuine engagement.
2. Mind the Length: Keep it concise; a lengthy comment can feel overwhelming. Save deeper conversation for DMs if she's receptive.
3. Use Emojis Wisely: A well-placed emoji clarifies tone. Too many can clutter your message. Strike a balance that feels natural.
4. Stay Respectful & Polite: Public comments are visible to others. Avoid anything overly personal or risqué unless you know she's comfortable with that.
5. Invite a Response: End with an open-ended question or a hint that welcomes her to continue chatting—online or in private messages.

By weaving creativity with genuine observation and compliments, you'll stand out as someone who truly notices and appreciates her content—paving the way for deeper, more personal connections. Enjoy exploring social media with charm and authenticity!

Chapter 15. Direct Messaging in Social Media

Below are 16 carefully crafted compliments, conversation hooks, or pick-up lines suited for Direct Messaging on Social Media. Since direct messages often begin with a personal, one-on-one dynamic, focus on her profile cues (interests, photos, or captions) and convey genuine curiosity. Let sincerity lead the way, with fun and warmth sprinkled throughout.

1. Cheeky

Line: "I was casually scrolling, but your profile turned my lazy afternoon into a much brighter moment—mind if I thank you properly?"

- Tone & Delivery: Lighthearted, a dash of playful gratitude.
- Adaptation: Great for a DM when you've just discovered something fascinating in her profile. You're

gently asking permission to engage more.

2. Cheesy

Line: "If profiles could win awards for making someone smile, you'd be holding a trophy right now."

- Tone & Delivery: Sweet, slightly over-the-top, but with a warm sense of humor.
- Adaptation: Perfect if her pictures or captions are genuinely uplifting or funny. Acknowledge her positive presence.

3. Corny

Line: "I tried to leave a witty comment, but I ended up just staring at your photos—I guess 'speechless' counts as a reaction, right?"

- Tone & Delivery: Friendly, with a short chuckle.
- Adaptation: Good if she has an engaging photo set that left you momentarily without words. Emphasizes genuine admiration.

4. Flirty

Line: "There's something about your vibe that screams 'awesome person alert.' Care to confirm my suspicions?"

- Tone & Delivery: Easygoing, playful confidence.
- Adaptation: Works if her bio or pictures hint at a fun or charismatic personality. You're indirectly asking her to share more about herself.

5. Phone-Related

Line: "My phone suggested it's time for a break, but your

profile is telling me otherwise. Let's see which one wins?"

- Tone & Delivery: Light, teasing—suggesting you're happily breaking your "phone rules" to talk to her.
- Adaptation: Ideal if you or she mentioned phone usage or digital detox. Shows you're making time for her.

6. Romantic

Line: "It's odd how a few images and words can spark such curiosity—I can't help but wonder what your story sounds like in person."

- Tone & Delivery: Soft, reflective, with genuine interest in who she is beyond the digital realm.
- Adaptation: Best if you sense a deeper vibe from her profile—maybe she posts thoughtful captions or has a creative flair.

7. Rude

Line: "You know, I was being super productive until your profile decided to hijack my attention—who do I contact about filing a distraction complaint?"

- Tone & Delivery: Smiling, sarcastic banter. Possibly add a winking emoji (\uD83D\uDE09) for clarity.
- Adaptation: Only if you see she's open to or has displayed playful sarcasm in her posts. Otherwise, it might be misinterpreted.

8. Crude

Line: "I'm trying to keep it classy, but you're making it tough. Can I at least admit you look amazing without breaking all decorum?"

- Tone & Delivery: Slightly daring but still polite. Keep it from sounding objectifying.
- Adaptation: If her profile has a bold, confident edge and you suspect she might enjoy a little spice in conversation.

9. Weird

Line: "If we lived in a parallel universe, I'd bet your profile would still be the coolest thing on the timeline. Care to bring that parallel world a bit closer?"

- Tone & Delivery: Quirky, imaginative. Use a playful emoji or two (\uD83D\uDC7E, \uD83E\uDD14) if you like.
- Adaptation: Ideal if she's into nerdy, whimsical topics or if she posts creative, offbeat content.

10. Lines Specifically for Women (to Use on Men or Other Interests)

Line: "Your bio left me curious—did you really think you could intrigue me this much and get away without a friendly interrogation?"

- Tone & Delivery: Confident, slightly sassy, but friendly.
- Adaptation: Perfect if his profile hints at interesting hobbies or cryptic statements. You're letting him know you want to know more.

11. Cheeky Redux

Line: "I noticed you're a fan of [shared interest]. I'd say let's team up, but I'm pretty sure you'd outshine me."

- Tone & Delivery: Self-deprecating humor, winking at her expertise.
- Adaptation: Reference a hobby or interest she's mentioned—travel, a sport, a favorite show—so it feels personal and relevant.

12. Cheesy Redux

Line: "They should add a new reaction button for your posts—something between 'Wow' and 'Where have you been all my life?'"

- Tone & Delivery: Very playful, acknowledging it's a bit grandiose.
- Adaptation: Great if she posts regularly and you genuinely love her content. It's a sweet exaggeration that shows appreciation.

13. Corny Redux

Line: "I have a feeling we could write one epic story—Chapter 1: This DM. Care to co-author something memorable?"

- Tone & Delivery: Bold, imaginative, framing your conversation as a potential adventure.
- Adaptation: Suited for someone who seems creative or open to the whimsical. A fun way to propose ongoing interaction.

14. Flirty Redux

Line: "You seem like the kind of person who turns ordinary moments into brilliant memories. I wouldn't mind tagging along for a few."

- Tone & Delivery: Warm, reflective, with genuine

intrigue.

- Adaptation: Ideal if she shares everyday life moments with a personal flair—you're acknowledging her ability to make life special.

15. Phone-Related Redux

Line: "My phone and I had a deal: less screen time. Then I found your profile... so, about that deal..."

- Tone & Delivery: Friendly, a bit self-mocking.
- Adaptation: Use if you're referencing a recent resolution or if she's posted about balancing digital life. It playfully shows you'd rather chat with her.

16. Romantic Redux

Line: "A few pictures and words can't possibly capture who you are, but they do hint at someone I'd love to know beyond the screen."

- Tone & Delivery: Genuine, calm, with a hint of longing.
- Adaptation: Great if you sense a real emotional or creative edge to her profile, letting her know you value deeper connection.

Tips for Success in DMs

1. Reference Something Specific: Tailor your line to her interests, photos, or captions. Show genuine curiosity about her.
2. Balance Compliments with Curiosity: Avoid over-flattery. Ask questions that invite her to share about herself—dialogue is more compelling than monologue.
3. Use Emojis to Clarify Tone: A well-placed smiley or wink can prevent misunderstandings, especially for

bolder lines.

4. Keep It Respectful: If she's slow to respond or seems uninterested, gracefully bow out or pivot to a lighter topic.

5. Focus on Authentic Engagement: Shifting quickly from a quick opener to genuine conversation is key. Show you're truly interested in who she is.

By blending these lines with attentive listening and thoughtful follow-ups, you can spark meaningful connections—turning ordinary DMs into something genuinely memorable. Enjoy your conversations!

Chapter 16. Wedding Receptions

Below are 16 carefully curated compliments, hooks for attraction, or pick-up lines suited for a Wedding Reception setting. Because wedding receptions celebrate love, the energy is typically upbeat and sentimental. Lean into the joyous mood, but maintain etiquette—keep your approach friendly and respectful, honoring the couple's special day.

1. Cheeky

Line: "I thought the bride and groom were the stars tonight, but then I saw you lighting up the room—care to share some of that spotlight?"

- Tone & Delivery: Lightly playful, with a genuine smile.
- Adaptation: Best used when she's clearly having a good time and radiating positivity. Compliment her presence without detracting from the couple's day.

2. Cheesy

Line: "They say weddings are all about love—but you just gave me a whole new reason to believe in happily ever after."

- Tone & Delivery: Warm, acknowledging it's slightly over-the-top with a soft smile.
- Adaptation: Great if she's demonstrated romantic enthusiasm for the wedding or made a sweet comment during the ceremony.

3. Corny

Line: "Between the couple's vows and your smile, my heart's on double overload tonight. Mind if I check in for a 'happily ever after' chat?"

- Tone & Delivery: Gently humorous, referencing the love-centric environment.
- Adaptation: Perfect if she's been genuinely moved by the ceremony, reinforcing the dreamy wedding ambiance.

4. Flirty

Line: "Of all the things I expected to enjoy at this wedding—food, music, dancing—I never guessed meeting someone like you would top the list."

- Tone & Delivery: Sincere, with good eye contact and a friendly grin.
- Adaptation: Use during a moment of shared laughter or post-ceremony conversation to highlight that she's an unexpected highlight.

5. Phone-Related

Line: "I took a ton of photos of the bride and groom, but the best picture here might be one of us—care to make that happen?"

- Tone & Delivery: Light, almost spontaneous, hinting at creating a fun memory.
- Adaptation: Ideal if you or she is snapping photos. Extend the invitation to share a moment together without being pushy.

6. Romantic

Line: "Watching them exchange vows feels magical—makes me wonder if a spark like that might be waiting for the two of us."

- Tone & Delivery: Soft, reflective, letting the wedding's romantic tone flow into your compliment.
- Adaptation: Ideal when the reception's mood is calm or heartfelt, like during slower dance music or post-dinner conversation.

7. Rude

Line: "This was supposed to be a low-key night of celebration... but then you walked in, and now I'm completely distracted—thanks for that."

- Tone & Delivery: Grinning, playful exasperation, clarifying you're joking.
- Adaptation: Use only if there's a light banter vibe. She should already seem comfortable and open to teasing.

8. Crude

Line: "I was trying to behave tonight, but you're not making it easy—temptation in a wedding dress code, if I've ever seen it."

- Tone & Delivery: Slightly daring but polite; don't let it sound too suggestive.
- Adaptation: Ensure she's comfortable with boldness. If there's any hesitation or formality, switch to a softer approach.

9. Weird

Line: "If this was a medieval wedding, I'd be your knight, sneaking away from the feast to chat under the moon. Up for a little modern twist on that?"

- Tone & Delivery: Quirky, delivered with a whimsical smile.
- Adaptation: Perfect if she has a quirky sense of humor or the wedding has a fun theme. A nerdy reference can break the ice if she's into it.

10. Lines Specifically for Women (to Use on Men or Other Interests)

Line: "Everyone's looking at the bride's stunning dress—but you're the one who's really got my attention. Think we could compare notes on this amazing evening?"

- Tone & Delivery: Friendly, confident, acknowledging the wedding setting.
- Adaptation: A direct approach that flips the script, giving you control while still being complimentary.

11. Cheeky Redux

Line: "I came here prepared to celebrate the newlyweds, but apparently, the real celebration is meeting you. Didn't see that on the invitation."

- Tone & Delivery: Light, acknowledging the wedding's official purpose.
- Adaptation: Use if you spontaneously ended up chatting and sharing laughs, highlighting how unexpected yet delightful the encounter is.

12. Cheesy Redux

Line: "The couple's love story is beautiful, but something tells me I just stumbled on another chapter worth exploring—care to co-author with me?"

- Tone & Delivery: Good-natured, romantic vibe.
- Adaptation: Mention how love stories are in the air, extending that possibility to the two of you.

13. Corny Redux

Line: "I thought the biggest sparkle would be the ring on the bride's finger, but your eyes are seriously giving it competition."

- Tone & Delivery: Delivered with genuine awe, but keep

a slightly playful edge.

- Adaptation: Great if she's wearing a glamorous outfit or has an especially bright, happy expression.

14. Flirty Redux

Line: "I see so many people dancing, but you've got a rhythm that's impossible to ignore. Mind if I catch that beat with you?"

- Tone & Delivery: A friendly invitation, leaning in with confidence but not pressure.
- Adaptation: Perfect for the dance floor portion of the reception. Connect music and dance with a personal invite.

15. Phone-Related Redux

Line: "I was snapping pictures of the newlyweds, but now I'm thinking the best memories tonight could come from a photo with you—selfie time?"

- Tone & Delivery: Casual, upbeat.
- Adaptation: Smoothly transitions from capturing the moment to focusing on the two of you. If she's already taking pictures, even better.

16. Romantic Redux

Line: "Weddings always remind me how beautiful it is when two souls connect—seeing you here, I can't help but wonder if fate has more in store for us."

- Tone & Delivery: Soft, reflective, eyes full of warmth.
- Adaptation: Ideal for a slower, more intimate moment, perhaps when the music calms or you're both enjoying a quiet corner.

Tips for Success at Wedding Receptions

1. Acknowledge the Occasion: Compliment the event, the bride and groom, or the ambiance before focusing on her. It shows respect for the day's purpose.
2. Observe Formality Levels: Weddings often mix different age groups and traditions. Keep your approach classy unless she clearly matches your playful or edgy banter.
3. Time It Right: Don't interrupt important moments like speeches, the first dance, or family interactions. Wait for a more relaxed phase of the reception.
4. Stay Positive & Gracious: Weddings are about celebration. Maintain a friendly, uplifting vibe, and be receptive if she wants to talk more about the couple or the festivities.
5. Transition Smoothly: If things go well, invite her to dance or share a toast. These are natural next steps at a reception, reinforcing the connection.

By delivering these lines with genuine warmth and a respectful nod to the couple's big day, you'll blend seamlessly into the romantic atmosphere, all while making her feel uniquely special amidst the celebration. Enjoy celebrating love—and maybe sparking a bit of your own!

Chapter 17. Family or Friends' Milestone Celebrations

Below are 16 carefully curated compliments, conversation starters, and pick-up lines that work well during Family or Friends' Milestone Celebrations—whether it's a birthday party, anniversary, graduation, or other special occasion. Because these events honor someone special (and often involve close friends and relatives), it's important to remain respectful while injecting just the right amount of charm and fun.

1. Cheeky

Line: "I came here ready to celebrate, but I didn't realize I'd be celebrating meeting you—think we can make this a party of two at some point?"

- Tone & Delivery: Warm, playful, with a smile that shows enthusiasm.
- Adaptation: Perfect if you've been talking or exchanging glances while everyone else focuses on the main honoree.

2. Cheesy

Line: "I thought the biggest reason to cheer tonight was [the celebrant's achievement], but now I'm clapping for the fact that you're here."

- Tone & Delivery: Gently acknowledge the cheesiness, but keep it sincere.
- Adaptation: Ideal if she's contributed to the positive atmosphere or if she's gone out of her way to support the person being celebrated.

3. Corny

Line: "Between all these heartfelt toasts and your bright smile, I'm feeling like this celebration just got even sweeter."

- Tone & Delivery: Genuine, with a small laugh to own the corniness.
- Adaptation: Great for a moment when everyone's making speeches or offering kind words. You segue from the general sentiment to a personal compliment.

4. Flirty

Line: "This event might be about someone else's milestone, but I can't help feeling like meeting you is my personal celebration."

- Tone & Delivery: Friendly, confident, with direct but respectful eye contact.
- Adaptation: Use after you've shared a few fun exchanges—let her see how her presence is a highlight for you.

5. Phone-Related

Line: "I was going to take a photo to capture this big day, but

I think the real picture I want is you, me, and a cool memory we can share. Up for it?"

- Tone & Delivery: Casual and spontaneous, like you just had the idea on the spot.
- Adaptation: Perfect if photos are being taken or people are updating social media. It naturally shifts from group memories to a more personal moment together.

6. Romantic

Line: "Watching everyone celebrate how special life can be makes me wonder—could this be the start of something special for us too?"

- Tone & Delivery: Soft, thoughtful, leaning into the event's sentimental vibe.
- Adaptation: Ideal for a calm moment—perhaps after a heartfelt speech—when emotions are already running warm and positive.

7. Rude

Line: "I was all set to just enjoy cake and small talk, but you had to come along and completely steal my focus. Care to make up for it with a real conversation?"

- Tone & Delivery: Light exasperation, a friendly grin, showing you're teasing.
- Adaptation: Use only if she's responded well to light banter before. The line should feel more like a charming complaint than actual rudeness.

8. Crude

Line: "They say every celebration has a guilty pleasure. I'm starting to think mine just might be talking to you."

- Tone & Delivery: Slightly daring, but keep it toned down enough for a family-friendly vibe.
- Adaptation: If she's been flirty or open to a bit of edge, it can work. Otherwise, steer clear to keep it classy.

9. Weird

Line: "If this were an alternate universe, I'd bet this party would still bring us together—some things are just meant to be."

- Tone & Delivery: Whimsical, with a small smile to emphasize the playful nature.
- Adaptation: Ideal if she appreciates imaginative references or has shown a quirky sense of humor.

10. Lines Specifically for Women (to Use on Men or Other Interests)

Line: "They're honoring one milestone tonight, but I think discovering you might be the bigger cause for celebration—care to make it official?"

- Tone & Delivery: Confident, a dash of directness.
- Adaptation: Flip the script and show that you're the one taking initiative—works if he's giving signals but hasn't made a move.

11. Cheeky Redux

Line: "I know we're supposed to congratulate [the honoree], but I think you deserve an award for making this night unforgettable."

- Tone & Delivery: Good-natured, focusing on how she's contributing to the event's positive vibe.
- Adaptation: Use if she's actively participating—like helping to serve, entertaining kids, or just making folks laugh.

12. Cheesy Redux

Line: "Between the balloons and decorations, you're the real pop of color that's brightening up this entire celebration."

- Tone & Delivery: Warm, playful, letting her know you see her impact on the atmosphere.
- Adaptation: Great if she's wearing a standout outfit or has a particularly vibrant personality.

13. Corny Redux

Line: "You know how everyone's here for the milestone? I think my milestone might be getting the chance to talk to you tonight."

- Tone & Delivery: Softly delivered, leaning into the sweetness.
- Adaptation: A sweet way to express that meeting her is as memorable for you as the main event is for the guest of honor.

14. Flirty Redux

Line: "The best celebrations always have that extra sparkle—tonight, I'm pretty sure that sparkle is you."

- Tone & Delivery: Confident but not overbearing. A warm smile seals the deal.
- Adaptation: Suited for when she's clearly enjoying

herself, dancing, or socializing comfortably.

15. Phone-Related Redux

Line: "I was planning to snap pictures of the big moments, but I realized the real highlight might be us sharing a candid one together. Up for it?"

- Tone & Delivery: Semi-spontaneous, focusing on creating a fun memory.
- Adaptation: If the family is taking pictures or you see her capturing moments, it's an easy pivot to suggest a quick selfie or photo together.

16. Romantic Redux

Line: "Seeing everyone celebrate life's sweet moments reminds me how special these connections are—I'd love to explore the possibility of one with you."

- Tone & Delivery: Gentle, heartfelt, showing real interest in building a bond.
- Adaptation: Ideal for a quieter moment when the party energy dips into more personal conversation— like after the cake's been cut or gifts unwrapped.

Tips for Success at Family or Friends' Milestone Celebrations

1. Acknowledge the Occasion: Compliment the guest of honor or the theme before shifting focus to her. It shows you're present for the shared celebration.
2. Show Polite Curiosity: Ask about her relationship to the host or the honoree. Personal connection can spark deeper conversation.
3. Maintain a Respectful Balance: Family or close friends

might be around. Keep your compliments warm, not overly sexual or intrusive.

4. Offer Genuine Compliments: Praise how she's contributing to the event's fun or supportive atmosphere, rather than just focusing on appearance.
5. Read the Room: If she's busy helping, talking to relatives, or engaged in the main event, pick a natural break to approach her.

By weaving these lines into a thoughtful, respectful approach, you'll charm her while honoring the milestone at hand—proving you can be simultaneously engaging, respectful, and ready to share in the joy of the celebration. Enjoy the party!

Chapter 18. Group Tours / Backpacking Hostels

Below are 16 curated conversation starters, compliments, and pick-up lines for Group Tours and Backpacking Hostels—settings where people come together from all over the globe to explore, connect, and share adventures. Here, openness and authenticity shine. Everyone's in discovery mode, so genuine curiosity about her background, travel stories, and personality can go a long way.

1. Cheeky

Line: "I heard this tour would open my eyes to new sights—guess they forgot to mention you'd be the most breathtaking view."

- Tone & Delivery: Bright, playful, a slight grin to acknowledge the flattery.
- Adaptation: Ideal if you've both just marveled at a scenic spot or historic site. Draw a contrast between the expected (the sight) and the pleasantly unexpected (her presence).

2. Cheesy

Line: "I came to explore a new place, but it seems the real discovery is meeting you—care to tell me more about your journey?"

- Tone & Delivery: Warm, intentionally a bit over-the-top, with genuine curiosity about her travels.
- Adaptation: Use if she's just mentioned her next travel plans or if you're swapping stories about how you each ended up here.

3. Corny

Line: "All these stamps in my passport, and I still feel like I've just arrived—maybe that's because meeting you feels like a whole new adventure."

- Tone & Delivery: Slightly self-deprecating chuckle, acknowledging it's a bit corny.
- Adaptation: Great if you've both collected travel stories or passport stamps. You tie in the idea that encountering her is a unique chapter in your travel

narrative.

4. Flirty

Line: "Between the hostel's laid-back vibe and your contagious energy, I'm pretty sure I found the best travel companion—even if it's just for a conversation right now."

- Tone & Delivery: Friendly confidence, making it clear you enjoy her presence without assuming too much.
- Adaptation: Perfect after a fun group activity (like a hostel game night) when you want to single her out for her good vibes.

5. Phone-Related

Line: "I've got a list of must-see sights on my phone, but I'm starting to think the top highlight is already right in front of me."

- Tone & Delivery: Lighthearted, referencing typical travel planning (maps, apps).
- Adaptation: If she's scrolling her phone or comparing travel itineraries, pivot to emphasize how she surpasses any recommended spots.

6. Romantic

Line: "It's incredible how two people from different corners of the world can meet in a hostel and spark such a connection—feel like exchanging a little piece of our stories?"

- Tone & Delivery: Soft, reflective. Let her see you value deeper conversation and genuine experiences.
- Adaptation: Good for a quieter moment, perhaps sharing coffee in the hostel common room or watching

a sunset together.

7. Rude

Line: "I was ready to just blend in with the group, but you had to show up and steal all the attention—seriously, not cool."

- Tone & Delivery: Light teasing, delivering a small grin or exaggerated eye-roll to signal you're joking.
- Adaptation: Best used if you've already shared some banter. She should be comfortable with a bit of push-pull humor.

8. Crude

Line: "Traveling is supposed to free the mind, but I can't seem to think of anything else but you right now. Care to help me release some of that tension?"

- Tone & Delivery: Slightly mischievous but keep it from crossing into disrespectful territory.
- Adaptation: Make sure the context is flirtatious and you already have rapport. Otherwise, it can be off-putting.

9. Weird

Line: "If this hostel was a spaceship traveling the universe, I'd definitely pick you as my co-pilot—wanna explore the unknown together?"

- Tone & Delivery: Quirky, with a playful smile that says you're fully aware it's an odd analogy.
- Adaptation: Perfect for someone with a fun, imaginative side or if you've had geeky/creative conversations (sci-fi, fantasy, etc.).

10. Lines Specifically for Women (to Use on Men or Other Interests)

Line: "I see you're collecting stories from every place you visit—I have a feeling your story might get even better if I join this chapter. Up for it?"

- Tone & Delivery: Confident, inviting.
- Adaptation: Flip the typical script; shows you're the one noticing him. Also leaves room for him to share more about his travels or next plans.

11. Cheeky Redux

Line: "They said group tours are about meeting new friends, but I'm starting to think my new favorite might just be standing right here."

- Tone & Delivery: Friendly, wide smile, acknowledging the group environment while singling her out.
- Adaptation: Good for a moment when you step away from the crowd to chat with her specifically—making it personal.

12. Cheesy Redux

Line: "I came for the local cuisine and scenery, but I didn't realize I'd find such a remarkable person to add to the menu of experiences."

- Tone & Delivery: Aware it's a bit silly, delivered with an appreciative grin.
- Adaptation: References discovering local culture and unexpectedly discovering her at the same time.

13. Corny Redux

Line: "I've got a map for almost everywhere I'm going, but no map could've prepared me for the route to your captivating smile."

- Tone & Delivery: Emphasize the playful pun—slight laugh or shrug.
- Adaptation: Great if you're literally pulling out a map or discussing directions. Tie it into her effect on you.

14. Flirty Redux

Line: "I'm not sure if it's the high altitude or just you, but my heart's racing a bit too fast. Mind if we slow down and talk about it?"

- Tone & Delivery: Friendly, direct, referencing the physical environment (like a mountain trek or a city known for high altitude).
- Adaptation: Perfect if you just finished a hike or you're in a location known for breathtaking views—blending the moment with your interest in her.

15. Phone-Related Redux

Line: "I was checking the best local hotspots on my phone, but something tells me the real highlight is a conversation with you—care to give me directions?"

- Tone & Delivery: Playful, letting her see you'd rather chat than rely on digital recommendations.
- Adaptation: Perfect for a quick break from scrolling or if she's glancing at her phone. A nudge toward real-life bonding.

16. Romantic Redux

Line: "Sometimes the most unforgettable moments happen between strangers on the road—do you think this could be one of them?"

- Tone & Delivery: Quiet, thoughtful, letting her sense your sincere interest.
- Adaptation: Great for a serene moment—like a picturesque sunset or a calm night at the hostel.

Tips for Success in Group Tours & Hostels

1. Embrace the Shared Adventure: Everyone's experiencing a new place together. Reference common experiences (the day's excursion, the bunk layout, local customs) to build rapport.
2. Gauge Her Comfort Zone: If she's in a large group conversation, ease in politely. If she's relaxing solo, approach with a friendly "How's the day been?"
3. Stay Respectful of Personal Space: Hostels often mean shared dorms or communal areas. Light compliments are fine, but be mindful of boundaries.
4. Offer to Team Up: Suggest exploring a local market or hiking a nearby trail together. Shared experiences create deeper connections.
5. Balance Humor & Genuine Interest: Light banter is fun, but also show genuine curiosity about her background, travel stories, and future plans.

By fusing these lines with active listening and an appreciation for the travel spirit, you'll create connections that feel organic, inclusive, and exciting—truly capturing the essence of a modern-day Casanova on the road. Safe (and enjoyable) travels!

Chapter 19. Airport Lounges or Waiting Areas

Below are 16 carefully chosen compliments, conversation hooks, and pick-up lines suited for the Airport Lounge or Waiting Area environment. Airports bring together people from all walks of life, often with limited time. A warm, genuine approach can create a memorable moment—even if you have just minutes before a boarding call.

1. Cheeky

Line: "I was worried my flight might be delayed, but seeing you here just made the wait worth every second."

- Tone & Delivery: Light and upbeat, with a playful glint in your eye.
- Adaptation: Perfect if she looks a bit bored or anxious about waiting. Acknowledge the inconvenience of delays while spinning it into a compliment about her presence.

2. Cheesy

Line: "I've been scanning the departures board, but I think

the real destination is a conversation with you—care to join me for a quick layover chat?"

- Tone & Delivery: Slightly self-aware grin; let her see you recognize the cheesiness.
- Adaptation: Use if you're both near the flight info screens or checking boarding times. Emphasize the idea of a friendly conversation pit stop.

3. Corny

Line: "They say airports are where stories begin—I'm pretty sure our story might start right here if you're up for it."

- Tone & Delivery: Delivered gently, acknowledging you're being a bit whimsical.
- Adaptation: Great for someone who seems open to serendipitous encounters, referencing the chance nature of meeting at an airport.

4. Flirty

Line: "I came here expecting a routine flight, but you just turned this terminal into the most exciting part of my journey."

- Tone & Delivery: Confident, but not overbearing. Flash a genuine smile to show your sincerity.
- Adaptation: Use if she's shown a friendly vibe—perhaps exchanging eye contact or a small smile from across the lounge.

5. Phone-Related

Line: "I was going to kill time scrolling through my phone, but I think chatting with you is a far better use of my battery."

- Tone & Delivery: Lighthearted, acknowledging how easy it is to default to phone use.
- Adaptation: Ideal if you notice her putting down her phone or glancing around—suggesting she, too, might be open to real conversation.

6. Romantic

Line: "It's amazing how two travelers can cross paths in the midst of all this chaos—makes me wonder if this moment is worth exploring a bit more."

- Tone & Delivery: Soft, reflective tone, with friendly eye contact.
- Adaptation: Perfect for a quieter corner of the lounge or during a lull in announcements, letting the environment's hum of activity contrast with the personal connection you're offering.

7. Rude

Line: "I was planning a peaceful wait until you distracted me with that captivating vibe—kindly explain how I'm supposed to focus on my flight now?"

- Tone & Delivery: Smiling exasperation, playful. Possibly add a small laugh or shrug.
- Adaptation: If she's responded well to joking or teasing before, it can land as fun banter. Avoid if she seems stressed or rushed.

8. Crude

Line: "Airports are all about security checks. I think you just triggered mine—any chance I could get a private screening of that smile?"

- Tone & Delivery: Bold with a mischievous smirk, but be ready to pivot if she's not into this style.
- Adaptation: Only if you've had a very flirty prelude, and she appears comfortable with edgy humor. Otherwise, opt for a gentler line.

9. Weird

Line: "If this airport suddenly transformed into a sci-fi portal, I'd definitely want you as my co-pilot to explore new dimensions—interested in an adventure?"

- Tone & Delivery: Quirky, with a playful sparkle that admits you know it's out there.
- Adaptation: Great if you sense she enjoys offbeat references or has a fun, imaginative streak (maybe reading a sci-fi novel or wearing something unique).

10. Lines Specifically for Women (to Use on Men or Other Interests)

Line: "I notice you keep checking the time—I have a theory you're just waiting for me to start this conversation. Care to prove me right?"

- Tone & Delivery: Confident, slightly mischievous.
- Adaptation: Perfect if you see him glancing at his watch or phone repeatedly, breaking the ice with playful confidence.

11. Cheeky Redux

Line: "They're announcing 'last call' soon, but something tells me the real last call should be me asking for your company—what do you think?"

- Tone & Delivery: A wink or friendly smile to convey

gentle humor.

- Adaptation: Use if your flight (or hers) is about to board. You're politely suggesting a chat in the last moments of waiting.

12. Cheesy Redux

Line: "I'm trying to figure out if the butterflies in my stomach are from takeoff nerves or that smile you just flashed—either way, I'm intrigued."

- Tone & Delivery: Good-natured, acknowledging it's a bit flowery.
- Adaptation: Perfect if she's expressing any nervousness about flying, or if you just exchanged a friendly glance.

13. Corny Redux

Line: "I bought a ticket for this flight, but meeting you feels like a bonus trip I never knew I signed up for."

- Tone & Delivery: Lightly enthusiastic, own the corniness with a small chuckle.
- Adaptation: Good if you've chatted a bit, making it clear you're pleasantly surprised by the connection.

14. Flirty Redux

Line: "It's ironic—we're all here trying to get somewhere, but now I kind of hope we could stay here talking a bit longer."

- Tone & Delivery: Sincere, with direct eye contact.
- Adaptation: Ideal if you're hitting it off and lamenting the limited time before boarding. Subtly suggests you value more conversation.

15. Phone-Related Redux

Line: "I was about to board with a playlist in my headphones, but your energy feels like the track I actually want to hear—mind if I listen a bit more?"

- Tone & Delivery: Friendly, referencing how you prefer real conversation over virtual entertainment.
- Adaptation: If she's also using headphones or flipping through a playlist, it's a natural pivot to person-to-person interaction.

16. Romantic Redux

Line: "Isn't it funny how an airport, a place of constant goodbyes, could offer the possibility of a beautiful hello between us?"

- Tone & Delivery: Warm, a bit reflective, letting her see you value chance connections.
- Adaptation: Best in a calmer moment, maybe after a light exchange. It gently invites her to consider what meeting you might mean.

Tips for Success in Airport Lounges & Waiting Areas

1. Respect Time Constraints: She may have a short layover or be heading to security. If she seems in a hurry, adapt accordingly or keep it brief.
2. Observe Her Cues: If she's engrossed in a book or appears anxious about her flight, consider a lighter approach or polite opener before a pick-up line.
3. Offer Assistance: If you see her looking for a gate, help out. Genuine acts of kindness can pave the way for natural conversation.

4. Be Mindful of Personal Space: Airport seats can be cramped. Keep your approach calm and friendly, never intruding too close without invitation.
5. Make Leaving Smooth: If one of you boards soon, gracefully exchange contact info or suggest continuing the chat if circumstances allow—no pressure.

By pairing these lines with genuine interest in her journey and a respectful sense of timing, you'll elevate the typical airport wait into a meaningful moment—proving that even in transit, a modern-day Casanova can find memorable connections. Safe travels!

Chapter 20. Elevator Chats

Below are 16 compliments, conversation openers, and pick-up lines suited for a brief Elevator Chat scenario. Elevators offer minimal windows for interaction—often a few seconds to a minute—so keep it light, respectful, and quick to adapt if she's not in the mood for conversation.

1. Cheeky

Line: "I came in here to go up a few floors, but it seems my day just went up a whole level after seeing you."

- Tone & Delivery: Light, friendly smile; let your voice convey slight amusement.
- Adaptation: Perfect for a subtle compliment that ties directly to the elevator ride.

2. Cheesy

Line: "I heard elevator rides can be awkward, but I think we just turned this one into a highlight of my day."

- Tone & Delivery: Slightly self-aware grin—acknowledge it's a bit over-the-top.
- Adaptation: Best if the elevator is not overly crowded; otherwise, it might feel intrusive. Ideal after sharing a quick smile or nod.

3. Corny

Line: "I'm starting to think the real express service here is how quickly you caught my attention."

- Tone & Delivery: A warm chuckle or small laugh, letting her see you know it's corny.
- Adaptation: Works well if the building has a fast elevator or "express" floors. Tie it into your compliment.

4. Flirty

Line: "I'm only going up a few floors, but I wouldn't mind if this ride lasted a bit longer, especially now that you're here."

- Tone & Delivery: Confident, but keep it soft and not too intense.
- Adaptation: Use if you make eye contact and sense

she's open to conversation. Keep it short in case you reach your floor soon.

5. Phone-Related

Line: "I was about to check my phone out of habit, but you're a far more interesting distraction—mind if I say hi instead?"

- Tone & Delivery: Light, with a friendly nod toward your phone, then back to her.
- Adaptation: Good if she or you were reaching for a phone. It invites a quick chat that can break the tension of standing quietly.

6. Romantic

Line: "It's funny how a few seconds in an elevator can feel special when you share it with the right person—like now."

- Tone & Delivery: Soft-spoken, sincere, brief eye contact.
- Adaptation: Ideal if the mood feels calm and you've exchanged a friendly glance.

7. Rude

Line: "I was looking forward to a peaceful elevator ride, but you had to show up and be this distracting... thanks for that."

- Tone & Delivery: A cheeky grin or playful eye-roll to show you're joking.
- Adaptation: Make sure she's smiling or open to banter. If she seems reserved or rushed, avoid this.

8. Crude

Line: "I came here for a quick lift, but I think my pulse just went sky-high, courtesy of you."

- Tone & Delivery: A slightly mischievous grin; keep it from sounding lewd.
- Adaptation: If you've already had a playful exchange or she's given bold signals, otherwise, safer lines might be better.

9. Weird

Line: "If aliens beamed us out of this elevator right now, I'd definitely keep you as my first contact—do you mind if I at least learn your name first?"

- Tone & Delivery: Quirky, with a soft laugh acknowledging it's out there.
- Adaptation: Great if she sports something unique—sci-fi T-shirt, unusual accessory—or if you've exchanged a playful vibe.

10. Lines Specifically for Women (to Use on Men or Other Interests)

Line: "You look like someone who knows how to make the most of a short ride—should we prove that by turning these next few seconds into a fun conversation?"

- Tone & Delivery: Confident, direct, with a friendly smile.
- Adaptation: Ideal for taking initiative. Shows you're comfortable striking up a quick chat in an unconventional spot.

11. Cheeky Redux

Line: "They say good things come in small packages—kind of like this elevator ride. But I have a feeling you could make it even better."

- Tone & Delivery: Friendly, referencing the smallness of the elevator.
- Adaptation: Perfect if the elevator is indeed small or if it's a well-known cramped space. Emphasize the playful tone.

12. Cheesy Redux

Line: "Who knew going up a few floors could feel like such a delightful climb, all because you're here?"

- Tone & Delivery: Slightly dreamy, acknowledging it's a sweet line.
- Adaptation: Suitable if she's in a good mood or you've already made eye contact. Keep it short because elevator time is limited.

13. Corny Redux

Line: "I was prepared for some elevator music, but it seems your presence is the real soundtrack I needed today."

- Tone & Delivery: Lighthearted, with a chuckle.
- Adaptation: Great if there's actual elevator music or if you're both commenting on the awkward silence. It's a corny ice-breaker.

14. Flirty Redux

Line: "I could list a hundred places where I'd love to meet someone interesting, but an elevator was never on that list—until now."

- Tone & Delivery: Pleasantly surprised, leaning in just enough to show interest, but not crowding her space.

- Adaptation: Use if she seems receptive, or if you have a few floors to go. It conveys a sense of happenstance in meeting her.

15. Phone-Related Redux

Line: "I was about to pretend to check my messages, but then I realized I'd rather engage with an actual person—would you mind if I said hi?"

- Tone & Delivery: Friendly, direct. Possibly glance at your phone before turning attention to her.
- Adaptation: Ideal if you or she is fiddling with a phone. It calls attention to the opportunity for real connection instead of phone-scrolling.

16. Romantic Redux

Line: "Strange how a mundane ride can feel like a fleeting moment of magic when I see you—makes me wish the doors wouldn't open so soon."

- Tone & Delivery: Gently heartfelt, meeting her eyes briefly.
- Adaptation: Perfect if the elevator ride is nearly over but you want to express admiration. End with a warm smile and maybe exchange contact info if the vibe is positive.

Tips for Success in Elevator Chats

1. Read the Situation: If she's engrossed in her thoughts or in a rush, a friendly "Hello" might suffice. Respect her space and time.
2. Keep It Short: Elevators are fleeting. A quick, pleasant comment can spark interest; extended monologues won't work.

3. Mind Personal Space: Stand at a respectful distance, especially in a tight elevator. Lean in only if she seems receptive.
4. Watch for Nonverbal Cues: If she smiles or engages, you can proceed. If she seems uncomfortable or nonresponsive, politely disengage.
5. Make a Gentle Exit: If you reach your floor or hers, gracefully wrap up: "Nice talking to you—hope the rest of your day is great!"

By matching your brief lines to the brevity of an elevator ride and wrapping them in genuine warmth, you can turn a mundane moment into a pleasant memory—showing that a modern-day Casanova can indeed find connection anywhere, even between floors. Enjoy your upward (or downward) journey!

Chapter 21. Public Transportation

Below are 16 compliments, conversation hooks, and pick-up lines tailored for Public Transportation—whether it's on a bus, train, subway, or tram. Because commuting can be hectic, it's important to stay observant and adapt quickly if she's not in the mood for conversation. Always prioritize respect and non-intrusiveness.

1. Cheeky

Line: "I thought rush hour was supposed to be the worst part of my day—then you got on board and changed my mind."

- Tone & Delivery: Friendly and slightly playful. Keep a warm smile.
- Adaptation: Ideal if she boards when it's crowded or stressful; you spin it into a positive note about her presence.

2. Cheesy

Line: "We're both going places, but somehow I feel the best direction is toward each other right now."

- Tone & Delivery: Gentle, acknowledging the sweet cheesiness with a small grin.
- Adaptation: Perfect if you make eye contact or share a quick laugh about a train announcement or bus delay.

3. Corny

Line: "I've noticed this bus is making all its stops, but I'm really hoping it doesn't stop me from getting to know you a little better."

- Tone & Delivery: A light chuckle, letting her see you're aware it's corny.
- Adaptation: Great if your bus has multiple stops. Ties in the travel theme, bridging to personal interest.

4. Flirty

Line: "This commute just went from ordinary to intriguing the moment you sat down—mind if I introduce myself?"

- Tone & Delivery: Polite confidence; easy smile and direct eye contact.
- Adaptation: Use if she chooses a seat near you or you're seated across from each other. Keep it short so she can decide if she wants to chat.

5. Phone-Related

Line: "I was about to put in my earbuds, but then I realized talking to you would be far more interesting. Care for a quick conversation?"

- Tone & Delivery: Warm, honest, referencing typical commuter behavior (tuning out on devices).
- Adaptation: Ideal if you or she has headphones in hand—shifting from isolation to engagement.

6. Romantic

Line: "Of all the journeys we take in life, the unexpected ones can be the sweetest—like meeting you on this train."

- Tone & Delivery: Soft, thoughtful, but not overly intense.
- Adaptation: Best for a calmer moment (e.g., outside of rush hour). Suggests a positive take on chance encounters.

7. Rude

Line: "I was trying to mind my own business, but you're making that impossible—seriously, how am I supposed to ignore a vibe like yours?"

- Tone & Delivery: A playful grin, showing exaggerated frustration.
- Adaptation: Only if she's open and playful herself. If she seems reserved or tired, a gentler approach is better.

8. Crude

Line: "They say commuting can be draining, but you've got me feeling all charged up—care to share your secret?"

- Tone & Delivery: Slightly daring but keep it from sounding vulgar.
- Adaptation: Observe her body language first. If she's tired or not smiling, skip this line.

9. Weird

Line: "If this bus magically turned into a rocket, I'd definitely pick you as my co-pilot—any interest in a cosmic commute?"

- Tone & Delivery: Quirky, playful. Let a small laugh show you know it's weird.
- Adaptation: Good if she has a whimsical or creative vibe (e.g., reading a fantasy or sci-fi novel).

10. Lines Specifically for Women (to Use on Men or Other Interests)

Line: "You seem like someone who knows how to make the best of any ride—mind if I join you for a few stops of interesting conversation?"

- Tone & Delivery: Confident, direct, but welcoming.
- Adaptation: Flip the script by approaching him; it shows you're sure of yourself and open to chat.

11. Cheeky Redux

Line: "I expected this train to take me to my destination, but I didn't realize it might also deliver me right into an intriguing conversation with you."

- Tone & Delivery: Lighthearted, referencing the journey.
- Adaptation: Good if you catch each other's eye after a delay or station announcement.

12. Cheesy Redux

Line: "I've heard about finding silver linings in everyday life—turns out the highlight of this trip might be meeting you."

- Tone & Delivery: A warm, slightly romanticized note.
- Adaptation: Perfect if you've shared a small laugh or moment about a common inconvenience (like a sudden stop or crowded train).

13. Corny Redux

Line: "My ticket says I'm going from A to B, but if you're up for it, maybe we can explore C (coffee) together sometime."

- Tone & Delivery: Friendly, with a hint of humor.
- Adaptation: Ties in her possible interest in coffee (or tea) as a low-key next step if the vibe is right.

14. Flirty Redux

Line: "The scenery outside might be a blur, but talking to you is the clearest highlight of this ride."

- Tone & Delivery: Calm confidence, direct eye contact, genuine smile.

- Adaptation: Use if you're seated side by side or facing each other, and you've had a moment to exchange a few glances.

15. Phone-Related Redux

Line: "I was scrolling social media, but I think I found a real-life upgrade right next to me. May I say hello?"

- Tone & Delivery: Light, acknowledging typical phone-scrolling.
- Adaptation: Great if you or she just looked up from a device—focusing on real interaction over digital.

16. Romantic Redux

Line: "It's rare to find someone who brightens a crowded bus like you do—care to share a bit of that light with me, if only for a few stops?"

- Tone & Delivery: Warm sincerity, gentle eye contact, short and sweet.
- Adaptation: Best if she exudes a positive aura or is in a good mood, so it feels like a natural compliment.

Tips for Success on Public Transportation

1. Mind the Setting: Space is often cramped, and people can be stressed. Start softly; gauge her reaction before continuing.
2. Check Body Language: If she's immersed in a book or wearing headphones, a polite "Excuse me" or wave can test if she's open to chatting.
3. Offer Help, If Appropriate: If she's struggling with bags or a seat, lend a hand first—acts of kindness can

pave the way for natural conversation.

4. Respect Boundaries & Time: She may get off soon or be in a rush. If she's not receptive, gracefully step back and wish her a good day.

5. Keep It Brief & Pleasant: Commuting is temporary. A short, sweet exchange can leave a positive impression without feeling forced or intrusive.

By delivering these lines with genuine politeness and staying attuned to her cues, you transform a potentially mundane commute into a chance for an enjoyable connection—proving once again that a modern-day Casanova can spark interest even on a busy bus or train. Safe travels!

Chapter 22. Dating Websites

Below are 16 tailored lines for Dating Websites, each grouped by type (cheeky, cheesy, corny, flirty, phone-related, romantic, rude, crude, weird, and lines specifically for women) and Redux options to keep things fresh. When messaging someone on a dating site, personalizing your opener to her interests or profile details significantly improves your chances of creating a genuine connection. Use these lines as a starting point, then add specific references to her bio, photos, or hobbies.

1. Cheeky

Line: "Your profile caught my eye like a stolen base in the last inning—may I congratulate you for the sneaky move?"

- **Tone & Delivery**: Playful, with a slight hint that she's done something impressive by capturing your attention.
- **Adaptation**: Perfect if she mentions sports or competitiveness in her bio. It subtly flatters her for being memorable.

2. Cheesy

Line: "I didn't think I'd find anything sweeter than my coffee this morning... then I saw your profile."

- **Tone & Delivery**: Acknowledge the sweetness factor with a small grin or cheerful emoji.
- **Adaptation**: Great if her photos exude warmth or if she mentions loving coffee. It's a short and sweet line that sets a positive tone.

3. Corny

Line: "I was just browsing, but now I'm convinced my search ends here—didn't realize I was looking for you all along."

- **Tone & Delivery**: Warm, letting her see you're aware it's a bit of a grand statement.
- **Adaptation**: Works if you sense a romantic vibe in her profile. Show you're confident but keep it light-hearted.

4. Flirty

Line: "You have this undeniable spark in your photos—I'd love a chance to see if it's just as radiant in conversation."

- **Tone & Delivery**: Confident but not pushy, acknowledging you're intrigued.
- **Adaptation**: Use if her profile pics suggest a lively personality. You're noting her "spark" and politely inviting her to a chat.

5. Phone-Related

Line: "I almost dropped my phone swiping right because your photos seriously knocked me off balance. Totally worth it."

- **Tone & Delivery**: Light, humorous, with a small laugh or playful emoji.
- **Adaptation**: Good if you want to compliment her looks in a playful way. Just keep it brief and respectful.

6. Romantic

Line: "Your profile reads like the first chapter of a beautiful story—I'm curious to see how the next pages might unfold."

- **Tone & Delivery**: Sincere, slightly poetic, reflecting genuine interest.
- **Adaptation**: Best used if she has a descriptive or creative bio. It shows you appreciate her depth.

7. Rude

Line: "I had this whole day planned for productivity, but you just sabotaged it by being far too interesting—well played."

- **Tone & Delivery**: Lightly exasperated, jokingly blaming her for your distraction.

- **Adaptation**: Only if her profile suggests she's playful or appreciates sarcasm. Make sure you end it with a friendly vibe.

8. Crude

Line: "People say looks aren't everything, but your profile is seriously challenging that notion—care to tell me what else you're working with?"

- **Tone & Delivery**: Bold yet not overtly disrespectful. Keep it a bit tongue-in-cheek.
- **Adaptation**: If her bio hints that she's direct or edgy, this may land. If unsure, choose a safer line.

9. Weird

Line: "If we were characters in a fantasy novel, I'd bet you're the one with the secret treasure map—I can't resist a good mystery. Care to share clues?"

- **Tone & Delivery**: Quirky, imaginative. Show you know it's an unusual analogy.
- **Adaptation**: Great if she's into nerdy/creative interests—fantasy, cosplay, or unique art. You're referencing her being intriguing.

10. Lines Specifically for Women (to Use on Men or Other Interests)

Line: "I see a lot of bravado on here, but I have a feeling you might be the real deal—want to prove my instincts right?"

- **Tone & Delivery**: Confident, direct.
- **Adaptation**: Excellent for flipping the script—your

approach displays self-assurance while inviting him to engage authentically.

11. Cheeky Redux

Line: "Your bio made me chuckle and your smile has me hooked. I'd say that's two reasons we need to talk—what do you think?"

- **Tone & Delivery**: Friendly, referencing something specific like her sense of humor.
- **Adaptation**: Perfect if she wrote something witty. It's a direct but easygoing invite to continue the conversation.

12. Cheesy Redux

Line: "Between your gorgeous profile pics and that witty tagline, I think I just found my new favorite online discovery."

- **Tone & Delivery**: Sweet, with a nod to how she stands out among countless profiles.
- **Adaptation**: Ideal if she has a compelling tagline or interesting quip in her bio.

13. Corny Redux

Line: "I was convinced my search would be endless—until your profile reminded me that happy endings might exist after all."

- **Tone & Delivery**: Warm, slightly dramatic, but with a playful grin or winky emoji.
- **Adaptation**: If she's expressed hope or positivity about dating in her profile, this can resonate well.

14. Flirty Redux

Line: "Your profile has this magnetism I can't ignore. Is it just as strong in conversation? Only one way to find out."

- **Tone & Delivery**: Direct, inviting her to prove the spark in chat.
- **Adaptation**: Use if you sense confidence or allure in her posts. Tread lightly if you're unsure of her comfort level.

15. Phone-Related Redux

Line: "Scrolling through dating profiles can feel like a chore, but you're the best interruption I've had all day. Care to chat?"

- **Tone & Delivery**: Casual, acknowledging the usual tedious swiping.
- **Adaptation**: A gentle approach that highlights how her profile genuinely stands out to you.

16. Romantic Redux

Line: "Seeing your passion for [shared interest] feels like a moment of serendipity—maybe we can turn this spark into a real-life adventure."

- **Tone & Delivery**: Soft, heartfelt, referencing a mutual interest from her bio.
- **Adaptation**: Best if you truly connect with something she mentioned (like travel, cooking, or a hobby). Show authentic curiosity.

Tips for Success on Dating Websites

1. **Personalize:** Reference something specific from her profile (photos, interests, quotes). Generic lines often

go unnoticed.

2. **Stay Respectful:** Jokes or mild sarcasm can work, but never cross into rudeness or pushiness.

3. **Balance Compliments & Curiosity:** Flattery gets attention, but also invite her to share about herself— ask open-ended questions.

4. **Gauge Tone & Reaction:** If she responds warmly, continue with thoughtful replies. If she seems cool or vague, gracefully pivot or give her space.

5. **Be Genuine:** Above all, sincerity resonates. Show genuine interest in who she is, not just how she looks.

These lines, combined with authentic curiosity about her profile details, create a warm and engaging first impression— helping you stand out and potentially leading to deeper conversations. Happy matching!

www.ingramcontent.com/pod-product-compliance
Lightning Source LLC
Chambersburg PA
CBHW020358130626
46549CB00006B/2338